Journeys Beyond

A series of interviews and discussions about meditation and spirituality

Kim Hughes

ISBN 978-0-9859480-0-9

First Edition, Second Printing

Garamond 12 point

Lexingford Publishing

New York

Ottawa

www.lexingfordpublishing.yolasite.com

Lexingford Series in Spirituality, Meditation, and Peace Studies

Foreword

So Babuji said, "We only look for lost things; we search for lost things." **God** is not lost. **I** am lost. Therefore, when I look, I am looking for my Self. Therefore, I am seeking my Self when I am meditating. When I find it, I find my Self. That is Self-realisation – the self, the ordinary mundane self, realising the higher Self which is its true Self – Self-realisation. (p. 105-106)

Rajagopalachari, Shri Parthasarathi (2005). *Heartspeak 2005*. Chapter on "Existence, Consciousness, Bliss."

Preface

This is the second in a series of books based on interviews with meditation practitioners. Abhyasis (followers) of Sahaj Marg meditation discuss how they became involved in spirituality and in this method, in particular. The spiritual master referred to in this book, affectionately known as Chariji, gave his permission for me to start this book in December of 2012. He passed on to the Brighter World just as the first book, *The Journey Within: Extraordinary Conversations with Uncommon People*, was published in late December of 2014. He was still bodily alive at the time these interviews were conducted and as the first drafts of the book were prepared.

This series of interviews and discussions about heart-based meditation and spirituality provided the opportunity to interview nearly 30 practitioners of the Sahaj Marg (Natural Path) meditation practice. Informants came from a variety of continents and cultures. They were mixed in age, gender and occupation. They also varied widely in their experience with meditation.

All but one of the interviews included in this book were conducted face-to-face at the headquarters for the Shri Ram Chandra Mission (SRCM) on the ashram grounds in Manapakkam, Chennai, India. Most were collected in July of 2013. Interviews typically lasted about one hour. All were recorded, transcribed, and checked for accuracy. One respondent elected to write her answers rather than conducting an interview. Minimal rewriting was done for fluency and cohesion. Brackets [ ] indicate additions by the writer.

This book is different from the first in the series as more advanced concepts are discussed and a number of advanced references are mentioned (e.g. Persian and Indian writers and saints); some traditional religious practices are discussed, as well. We also get a glimpse into the lives of people who have been involved in the meditation practice for decades. They give us much to consider about commitment, dedication and character development. Their words are both motivating and wise and their experiences profound. I hope you will enjoy this book and will share and discuss it with others.

Meet Kim Hughes (Huz)

Dr. Kim, as she is known by her students, has been a language educator and teacher trainer for over 30 years, living and working over half her life overseas. She and her family lived one year in Hong Kong, four years in Malaysia (where her second son was born), one year in Indonesia while on a Fulbright Senior Fellowship, and now 13 years in Macau. She has also lived and worked for shorter periods as a consultant in Austria and Japan. Kim was a tenured professor at Southern Illinois University in Carbondale for a decade in the 1990's and, at the time this book was written and published, employed at the University of Macau, S.A.R. China.

Although she has conducted and published academic research, this is Kim's second step into publishing for the general public. Her first book in the Lexingford Series in Spirituality, Meditation and Peace Studies, *The Journey Within: Extraordinary Conversations with Uncommon People* (2014), met with widespread and international reader acclaim, as evidenced by the book's amazon.com reader reviews. She started both book projects as someone new to meditation who wanted to learn more and to share what she had learned. Stress release, peace of mind, and lower blood pressure are but a few of the benefits she has noted personally. She was curious to learn if others had similar experiences. Seemingly, although a meditation "practice," this approach was becoming for her a "lifestyle," which was unexpected.

At that time, there was very little information available for people before actually starting the practice. She thought that the insights shared here (and in the first book of the series) would help both newcomers and those more experienced.

In her leisure time, Kim enjoys spending quiet time with her husband of over 30 years and their two sons, both in their mid-

20's. She enjoys travel, cooking, reading and learning languages. Increasingly, more and more of her personal time is oriented toward meditation on the heart.

Acknowledgments

Our beloved Master and my Tender, Chariji Maharaj.
His successor in the earthly realm, Master Kamleshji D. Patel.

All the brothers and sisters who were willing to be interviewed
for this book.

Meditation Brothers and Sisters

Michelle-Elaine Sidwell and Claire Gormley, without whose
enthusiasm, connections and support this book never would
have happened.

Hari Venkatesan, Judith Polston, Martin Worthy, Susan Leroux
Navarro and Alice Tesler for advice and expertise.

Sister Elizabeth Denley, for her kind help, affectionate support,
unflagging energy and attention to detail.

Family and Relatives

Betty Lou (mother) and Tom (husband), with special thanks to
their editing pencils and their loving hearts. Devin, Renata,
Kelsey and Joana (dear sons and daughters of my heart), much
love and happy reading. Kaye (sister) and Bruce and Craig
(brothers) and their families. Terry and Greg, Jim (in-laws) and
our wonderful nieces and nephews.

Marion Hughes (father), Tony and Pat Wilhelm, Joey Wilhelm,
Peggy Quirk, Mary Wilhelm, and Sean Beall, watching over us
from the Brighter World.

Hari and Anu Venkatesan, Joseph Sommerville and Marie
Mater, Terry and Ellie, Vicki and Tang, Rando and Mike,
Faridah and Charles, Manuela and Tony, Kelly and Kris, the

Frenches, the Bobays, the Bodnars, the Caldwells, Robbey Byers, Chris Backs and Eric, Alan and Cathy, Gloria Ulloa, April Bonar, Stephanie Lam, Susan Krieg, Gala and Konstantin, Glenn Timmermans, Nina and Gary, Teresa Lacuna, and Bill Guthrie for being true-blue, forever friends.

Art Bell and Dayle Smith, for believing in this project.

The production staff of Lexingford Publishing for making this dream a reality.

Dedication

Dedicated to my husband and family. Thank you for sharing your lives and your love with me. Thank you, dear Tender Chariji Maharaj and Rev. Kamleshji, for your approval and support of this project as well as your blessings, guidance and love for us all.

Table of Contents

Introduction

In the first book of this series, *The Journey Within: Extraordinary Conversations with Uncommon People* (2014), we heard from sixteen interviewees who discussed how to get started in a meditation practice. They also discussed a number of lifestyle changes to consider or anticipate, and commented on their personal relationships with and the role of a spiritual master. We heard from people who have made spirituality the focus of their lives and we learned how their goals are operationalized in everyday life. We learned of hopes and dreams for a future where we respect our planet and other living beings.

Similar themes continue in this, the second in the series, but this text is, at the same time, a bit more advanced. (Please see the final section of the book for references and resources mentioned throughout.) People already in the practice will particularly enjoy some of the stories and experiences shared here. In this book, for example, we meet several people who were among the first Westerners (Occidentals) to travel to India to meet Shri Ram Chandra, affectionately known as Babuji. Babuji is also known as Ram Chandra of Shahjahanpur and was founder president of Shri Ram Chandra Mission (SRCM). Now thirty to forty years in the practice, these abhyasis (followers) reminisce about Babuji's teachings, his humility, and their own experiences as young people delving into spirituality. They discuss important concepts such as liberation, surrender, mergence, and constant remembrance. These interviewees bring decades of experience as prefects or preceptors (see glossary, which follows) and give sound advice and true "pearls of wisdom" for newcomer seekers.

It is fascinating to hear from several of our Indian sisters and brothers as they discuss their family upbringings, religious and spiritual experiences, reactions to some of the traditional practices taught by their families or in-laws, and personal fulfillment on their paths to spiritual development. It is interesting to put ourselves in their shoes as they discuss indoctrination by family and society, arranged and love marriages, raising children in the Sahaj Marg way, and contributing by service to their mission. Several mention in loving detail their search for a guru and talk with wonder at their good fortune to find such a loving and tender Master in Babuji's successor, affectionately known as Chariji, the Revered Parthasarathi Rajagopalachari.

You will also meet a diverse mix of people from all over the world, including Algeria, Australia, France, India, Iran, Spain, the U.K and the U.S.A.. All share the same message, that we need to foster love in our hearts. We are sisters and brothers and we need to learn how to tolerate and respect each other. Only if we change ourselves can we change the world. For each of us, our only real job is to work on ourselves, learning how to grow and evolve spiritually. I hope you will find these stories to be thought-provoking, interesting, and insightful. I imagine you re-reading these stories and sharing favorite sections to discuss with others as a means to explore your own journeys within and beyond. Happy reading!

Glossary of Terms

If not sourced, definitions are taken from:
https://www.sahajmarg.org/literature/glossary

abhyasi: a follower of Sahaj Marg meditation practice; practicant of Sahaj Marg

acharya (aachaarya): religious teacher

bhandara: a gathering or banding together, usually for a celebration such as the birth or death anniversary of one of the Masters; typically 2-3 days under open tents

bhakta: devotee (follower from the heart)

bhog or **bhoga (bhogaa)** or **bhogam**: The process of undergoing the effects of impressions; experience; enjoyment.

chakras: in Hindu and tantric/yogic traditions and other belief systems chakras are energy points or knots in the subtle body. They are located at the physical counterparts of the major plexuses of arteries, veins and nerves. From http://en.wikipedia.org/wiki/Chakra

devi: goddess

devta: one who gives selflessly. Also see http://yogsadhanashram-usa.org/2011/04/devtas-what-is-a-devta-how-many-are-there-who-are-they/

karma: the Pali term Karma literally means action or doing. Any kind of intentional action whether mental, verbal, or physical, is regarded as Karma. It covers all that is included in the phrase "thought, word and deed." Generally speaking, all good and bad action constitutes Karma. See http://www.buddhanet.net/e-learning/karma.htm#1

pranam: respectful salutation; obeisance, usually made through pressing the palms together and raising to the chest or forehead

prasad or **prasadam (prasaad or prasaadam):** divinized food, usually sweet; an offering to Master or God

prefect(or), precept(or): one who draws upon Divine energy, working through the living Master, to assess the abhyasi's condition and help by transmitting energy, peace, and whatever else is needed

puja (poojaa): religious traditional practice; in Sahaj Marg, the meditation practice

pundits: scholars

quantic therapy: See http://www.gilles-placet.com/

rishi: seer, saint

sadhana: the practice, in all its components

Sahaj Marg: the 'Natural Path,' a simple practice of meditation on the heart derived from the ancient Indian system of raja yoga. "The true aim of this highly effective training in spirituality is to take the seeker to the highest goal of human existence: God realization or Self realization." Please see www.sahajmarg.org

samskaras: impressions from this and past lives, which can inhibit the soul's evolution if not removed

sahaj samadhi (sahaja samaadhi): natural samadhi, considered the highest samadhi: simultaneity of total external awareness with total inner emptiness or absorption

samskara(samskaaraas): impressions; grossness

sannyasi/n (sannyaasi/n): One who has renounced the world and leads a solitary life of celibacy and asceticism

satsang: spiritual assembly; being with reality

sitting: a session of meditation, usually lasting from 30 minutes to an hour, in which the Master or a prefect/preceptor meditates with a group or an individual for the purpose of cleaning and transmission

Chapter 1

Evolved Science Fiction

Jean Michel

mid 60's, male, French, therapist

Preface: I had the good fortune to have met Jean Michel on several occasions by the time we conducted the interview at our friend's apartment. In fact, we stayed at the same guest house and enjoyed several meals and walks together on one of my visits. He is a dignified older French gentleman with a lovely sense of humor, a strong sense of compassion toward others, and a love of good cuisine. He was involved with the university community in France and dabbled in the study of parapsychic phenomena while still a young man. He was the first to invite the second Master of the practice, Babuji Maharaj, to Europe and thus was instrumental in getting ashrams started in France and, indeed, all over Europe.

Our friend serves tea and biscuits and makes herself available as a translator. He turns to her for the occasional word as we conduct the interview, which is light-hearted and convivial even though we cover a lot of ground and had several people sitting in to listen. They are interested to hear what Jean Michel has to say because he is one of the first Occidental Europeans to start the Sahaj Marg meditation practice, among the first to visit Babuji in India, and the first to invite Babuji to the West. He speaks to us about the early days of the mission, about his relationship with two Masters, and about overcoming his fears of death and dying. Saying that his life in Sahaj Marg goes beyond any science fiction, Jean Michel shares with us his story and his encouragement to be yourself and to show yourself as you truly are.

Kim: We are here with Jean Michel, and this is a treat because it is my understanding that he is the oldest abhyasi from Babuji's time. Is that right?

In fact, I am the second oldest. I was introduced to Sahaj Marg around 1971 and helped to organize the first visit of Babuji to the south of France in May of 1972. I was in charge of organizing the meetings in Nice. We prepared a small meditation hall (the "ashram") and we organized a flat in a home with a big garden. We gave some lectures and radio interviews before Babuji's visit. When he came for those few days, many people came to visit him.

Kim: Could you tell a little about your background? Were there any formative experiences growing up that made you interested in spirituality?

I was born as a Christian Catholic and was very involved in Christianity before the age of twelve. It was very important to me then, but, at age 12, I became a refugee from Algeria to France. After the war, I did not want to hear about religion or God because I did not see the justice in losing everything in one day, losing my home and [fleeing to] a foreign country.

The first sense of spirituality came when I was 18, but I didn't understand that spirituality was something different to religion. So I started reading and attended organized lectures to understand. I became quite interested in Buddhism and had encounters with people from Tibet involved in it [Buddhism].

Kim: What was special about age 18?

To be frank, I was more interested in flying saucers and early civilizations, just like many of my age. We read a lot of books about Tibet like The Third Eye by Lobsang Rampa (1956) and other things. I was born in 1949, so it was 1968, 1969. I was looking for some existential answers - the "whys." We had been meditating for over a year but we did not know it was a transmission and we didn't know about cleaning. We didn't know anything about prayer, so we just had meditation. Babuji was happy to have a meditation, a meditation hall, and people to work with in Europe.

Kim: What was your impression of Babuji?

I first met Babuji when we went to organize the food and other things. From the very beginning, I felt he was something different. He was so sweet, so caring. He was as light as a feather. Everything was so nice with him. After a few days at the hall, Chariji told me that Babuji wanted to talk to me. When I went down to see him, he asked me if I would like to work with him. I told him that I would. I had done many things for other organizations and I agreed. I asked him what this concerned. He said that it was very simple. It was to uplift the spiritual level of humanity. It was almost like I had flushed the toilet and the whole roof crashed on to my head!

So he told me that I would work with him and he gave me individual sittings. On the last day, he told me to fast. The day of his departure, he told me that I could start my work, but I asked him what it was. He told me that I should give meditations and transmit. I said, "Transmit what?" He said just to sit in front of the people and imagine it is him giving the meditation and that I could even put his hat on my head, and he told me that I would see it starting. As he gave me his business card, he told me I would be welcome to come and stay with him if I wanted to know more. This was in January of 1972; in August I bought a flight and went to India.

In a way, things were easier in the past because we worked without knowing anything and the work was ongoing. There were no preceptor meetings, no meetings on how to work on people and meetings on how to help people. Today there are so many seminars about so many things. Back then, we just welcomed the people to the work and it worked very well.

Kim: I know the Mission didn't even exist at that time, and I was wondering how it has changed over time. You can comment on that or not, as you wish.

I would not like to get nostalgic about the "good old days," but when you visit your Master and there are only three or four foreigner abhyasis and, from morning to night, you are living in the same house as your Master – you see him reading his paper, smoking his hookah – the relationship was so very different. It can be frustrating when you now have 10,000 people and you are in a queue for several hours over a few days to greet your Master, when you know this is the only way to make contact. However, it's also good to learn to be free of the physical Master.

Kim: How have you changed since becoming an abhyasi?

I think I have changed, as I was very anxious and I was afraid of death. For many, many years, not one day would pass that I would not be thinking of my death. That was quite difficult to live with. I was also quite shy. In my job, I [now] give a lot of lectures. This ability that I now have is a gift from my Master. This is all to do with Master; that's for sure.

Beyond that, I had a few experiences (not that many) but when you first realize what transmission is, it's like breathing oxygen for the first time. I used to wonder how I could have lived without oxygen in my past, so it was like a re-birth, breathing this spiritual energy.

Kim: Can you explain transmission? Is it explainable?

Transmission is like having a tube… you open the ends and the energy just flows in to the heart. So sometimes you apply your will to give the transmission and you are active in the work of cleaning and transmission. Sometimes you're like a radio, tuning in to "Radio Sahaj Marg" and you receive the program. I was in Turkey once, in Istanbul. I had just arrived and only had time to sit on my bed before I was submerged by transmission. I could not stop the transmission. Afterwards I had a report with Chariji and he said that yes, your Master has used you to do the work for that region. I don't know about other preceptors, but for me this is what it was like.

Even though I've been a preceptor for 27 years, I'm not the best example of a preceptor. Sometimes I'm a rebel in the Mission. On occasion, I like to drink champagne. Even when I was in Chennai, I used to go and eat fish. I like good things and am a bit of a gourmet. [*Author's note: According to* Essentials for Spiritual Trainers, *SRCM preceptors do not drink alcohol. The consumption of flesh is also discouraged and purity is emphasized.*]

My wife worked as a private secretary for the Consul General at the U.S. Embassy. During a party, I met a lady and we were talking together with a glass of champagne while the transmission was going on. She then became an abhyasi and later was one of the first preceptors in China (P.R.C.).

Kim: I wonder if you could talk a little bit about traveling with Babuji?

I was fortunate in having known Babuji before 1974 when his health began to deteriorate, but in 1972 and 1973 he was alert. When he came to France in 1972, he had to cancel a trip to visit different groups in India. The local people were so disappointed. When I visited India that first time, I was asked if I would be willing to join Babuji to take the trip that he had cancelled. I agreed and we visited different centers riding in a jeep. The road was difficult, but Babuji was okay with doing that because his health was still good. I had to give a speech in

English but my English was very poor so I had to translate it from French to English and then from English to Hindi. I also had the privilege of being garlanded (honored by having flowers hung around the neck) on arrival at each place, so it's a nice memory.

Kim: Did you ever seek or have any proof that Babuji is divine?

Yesterday I spoke about some events that could be considered miracles. When we travelled in a Volkswagen from France and passed through Iran, Afghanistan and Pakistan, we had to make special arrangements with the automobile club and there were rules about selling the car.

The engine broke down after we visited Master in India and we were unable to continue to Nepal, so we had to find a way to have the car repaired. We could not return to France with the car in that condition. Some Belgians offered to get us back to New Delhi and gave us 48 hours to sell the car. We went to Katmandu, put a "Car for Sale" flyer on the window and, within one day, we had a French couple who were interested but they had no money at the moment. I told them they had 24 hours to find the money. They said they were friends of the king of Jordan and that they would get the money. They had met the king while waterskiing, and they became friends. The king was the head of the automobile club of Jordan. They got the money and we then were able to go back to France after selling the car. That was more than just a coincidence.

Another time, I had some difficulty with my airplane ticket but things that seem impossible become possible when you follow the Master. When you are 48th on the waiting list to board his plane, and yet you get a seat, it's a bit funny. We all have experiences of small miracles like this.

But the real miracle of Sahaj Marg is transformation; this is the real growth. It's like hair growth. When you look in the mirror each day you won't see the hair growing, but if you were to see yourself in the mirror after one month, you see the growth. I have met others like the Dalai Lama and Sai Baba and did not feel anything, so I always returned to Babuji.

Kim: Would you have any advice for someone who is new to spirituality?

I think if I had to give advice to anyone, not only in Sahaj Marg, it is to be yourself and even more so in front of the Master. It is the job of the Master to change you. He "waters" the seed you bring. We should try to be ourselves under all circumstances, so he can see the good and the bad. He sees everything anyway. Just try to be yourself, that's all.

Sahaj Marg is a process of meditation, cleaning and prayer. Some people may have difficulty accepting prayer because it is a word connected with religion. However, we don't pray to get something. Prayer is an offering of your heart. When you meditate, when you pray and when you clean, you live in constant remembrance of something higher than you, that you can call divine. But even the word "divine" can be suspicious, so we can adapt any vocabulary to introduce spirituality without calling it "spirituality." You can talk about self-development. It's like some people live on the ground floor and don't even know there are higher levels or upper floors. So all you can do is ask them to open the door and experiment, ask them not to have prejudices.

Kim: I am a new abhyasi and live in a previously Portuguese colony. Everybody drinks wine, most people smoke and most eat meat. What can I tell people who enjoy their lifestyles? Why do we have to give up anything, or do we?

Babuji never asks for you to enact any changes; it just works by suggestion. I think your body will tell you when it is no longer interested in meat or alcohol. But it is better to take some time because frustration is worse than the rules you impose on yourself. The consent and commitment should come from within, not be imposed by external rules. It takes time and Nature gives us time; we should not have to renounce anything. But your transformation will bring you to another way of living and thinking. You will also slowly change your relationships – but the process is within you. I told you before that I am a rebel, that I won't do something that I don't want to do. If I am made to do something, I will react. So the consent should come from within.

Kim: Could you talk a little bit about Whispers, and how did all that happen? The audience knows nothing about it.

I am often asked about this. I have known a person who is a medium for many years. She was a friend and I was her preceptor when she lived in Cannes. She loved Babuji. He was everything for her. She received messages from Babuji [after his death] but didn't dare talk about it. I was interested in parapsychology and told her she definitely had to speak about it.

The first film of the Mission is "He Who Loves All." We used to watch this with her and a few other people in our center. Many people felt the meditation by just watching the film. I told Babuji, saying that when I show my film, people fall into meditation and feel the transmission. He said that I was correct.

Kim: She was a medium for Babuji to send messages from the brighter world and those messages are now published in The Whispers books. Was she a medium for other spirits also?

Yes, she had some contact [with other spirits], including her late husband who became an abhyasi on the "other side." So you see, if you try and introduce people to the Mission in this life and they don't stay, perhaps they will become abhyasis in the afterlife! Babuji says that even if they stop after the three introductory sittings, they will get the benefit at re-birth. It is possible to evolve spiritually even if one doesn't meditate.

Growth is the law of the universe. We do not [have to] wait for Sahaj Marg for evolution, but it is a short cut.

Kim: Could you expand on that a little bit? Nobody has talked about evolution as a law of the universe.

Chariji has spoken many times about evolution. It's a law of nature that everything has to grow and to die. So we are in this process and planet Earth is in this process and so is the solar system in the galaxy. If you accept this law of the universe, you understand that you cannot escape [death]. I mentioned before about all I had been through with the anxiety I had about death. You begin to understand that these laws are not against us but [instead are] our friends in our evolution.

In Sahaj Marg, you understand that the key to evolution is love. When you have a loving Master, it is so contagious that you start understanding what love is. So we are fortunate that we are on the path to opening the heart. The energy we see on the path is just an expression of love, that's all, and the gas is free. If you don't receive [aren't open to] the transmission, it could become extinguished; you can cut or block this "oxygen source."

The purpose of life is not to be old and die old. The butterfly can have successive lives, even after a week. I am not looking at being old. I just try to be in the "here and now" and enjoy it, even though sometimes it's difficult. I am waiting with hope to see these big changes on the planet because the system is very corrupt with this new religion of money. Now there is injustice. You have the poor and the rich and that is not fair. [Instead], we have to share everything.

Babuji said that atomic power was a wrong choice for humankind. I remember he said that there is on planet Earth a free and clean energy that has not yet been discovered. So maybe this will be the energy that will be freely available to all of humanity.

Kim: Do you feel as an abhyasi we all have an obligation to evolve human beings or is our main obligation to evolve ourselves?

For me the first obligation is to be coherent in regard to your level of consciousness. You have to adapt your way of life to your own thinking. So, you don't go to Mass on Sunday and show off your jewelry and then (only the seventh day), you give money to the poor. You don't exploit others. If you are coherent, there are many attitudes that are coherent with regard to other people. I don't think there is a rule. There are as many rules as there are people and we should have no judgment.

Kim: Do you have anything else to add?

In a quiet place, with a small group, Babuji is always here.

Kim: So do you still have a fear of death?

No. Sincerely, no. It has become a friendly thought now. I could give you Chariji's last answer. The last time I came to India, I asked Chariji, "Are you impatient to pass?" He said, "No, but I am very curious about having the experience." So I too am very curious about having the experience, and the experience will come in time, here or there. I have postponed many things. I just try to be ready when the time comes, and I wish you the same with all that.

Kim: Thank you. I've been thinking about that and want to make sure I don't waste any time while I'm here, right?

Yes. Here and now. *The Power of Now* (Tolle, 2004) is also a good book to read. We should not limit ourselves to Mission books. We should be open to read, meet and listen to other people. [It's important to emphasize that] we don't have to renounce anything. We have a living example of Chariji as someone who was successful in business. He flew with two wings, spiritual and material. Chariji says that we have to earn money, but money is not the purpose of life. If it allows you to come and visit your guru once a year, there's no harm in having money.

Kim: About the next Master - should there be any concern at all about a transition that is likely to occur in the next few years? Master is getting older.

Babuji says that there is only one Master, so if we realize who is the Master and try to connect yourself to the Master we should all be happy. Times will be difficult but also the reverse. Happiness will also be there.

I left my religion. Jesus was supposed to be the only one. When I read some biographies of Jesus, I liked his humanity and he opened the way. However, if he was the only representative of God, it closed the door; we could not reach his level. When Babuji came to France in 1972 he said, "I have not come to make abhyasis. I have come to make Masters." So it's not a problem to accept that a man can become divine. Otherwise, there is always separation and no possibility of becoming divine. The essence of the soul is divine; it's pure and it is in the light. The practice of meditation is just to develop more qualities as a human being. Perfection is already there and we are all divine.

Kim: It's kind of a lot to swallow that human beings are divine, reincarnation, spirit world. A lot of people have trouble with those concepts.

Yes. So they can start with science fiction and they will go beyond. As Einstein said, "Only the fantastic can have a chance to become true." So we are evolved science fiction. Babuji says that God is the exaggeration of reality. So the next step is reality. Spirituality is not the main purpose. [We should be] always going further, growing more.

Chapter 2

No End to Miracles

Joshna

Indian, female, late 40's

Preface: I was told I should interview Joshna as "she does a lot for the mission." Personally, I wanted to interview her because I learned she is a full-time housewife and mother who helps her husband in business while doing a great deal of service as a prefect and meditation trainer. She sounded like an amazing woman. We hadn't met before arranging the interview, but I immediately felt comfortable and welcome upon arriving at her home nearby the ashram back gate. Both she and her husband greeted me warmly, I was offered a cool drink, then we left her husband with his friend in the front room as we found a quiet place to talk. From the time we settled into her guest room to talk, I was mesmerized with Joshna's personal story. I emerged well over an hour later still caught in the spell of her narrative.

Joshna shares a number of experiences that not only helped her to grow in spirituality but provided the proof she needed as a basis for faith in her Master and in the system. This was particularly important for Joshna, who had already tried three religions before joining Sahaj Marg. Her experiences help us realize how connected the physical world is to the spiritual realm. Her devotion, blind faith and ability to surrender are heart-touching. She begins the interview by saying that, before she shares some of her most memorable experiences as a Sahaj Marg abhyasi, she would like to share a few words her Master once shared with her. He said, "Never force yourself, and let everything happen naturally. Does the fish know that it's in the water? Never force yourself; let everything happen naturally."

Kim: Your quote from Chariji makes sense, especially since Sahaj Marg is the Natural Path, right? I wonder if you could tell us a little about your background and influences growing up?

I was born in Dimapur, Nagaland (far northeast India) to a family with two religions: my father was Jewish and my mother a Christian. We are a family of three sisters and one brother. As a child, I would visit the (Christian) church every morning for service and was active in the choir but I also attended the Sabbath prayer (Jewish service) religiously every Friday. This is how the journey of my life started – fully dedicated to two religions because I never wanted to upset either of my parents.

At the age of 13, the most heartbreaking incident took place in my life when I lost my beloved father. I could have taken this loss positively or negatively. Fortunately, I took it positively, which made me a more responsible and sensitive individual. Even as an immature child, I never indulged myself in unwanted activities. As my brother was the eldest it was naturally his duty to take care of us but unfortunately, he could not carry out his duty. So I convinced myself that I had to be a living example for my mother and siblings by living my life righteously.

I got married at an early age of 19 into a Punjabi Brahmin family. It was a love marriage. Even though my husband and I were from different religious and caste backgrounds, we convinced our families and got married. We shared a beautiful bond and, even after 26 years of marriage today, we continue to have the same strong bond. At the time we got married, we understood each other's responsibilities and respected them.

My mother-in-law was highly religious and devoted, following orthodox practices that sometimes seemed superstitious. It took her some time to accept me but the day she accepted me for who I am, she revealed a different side of her nature, one of protector and mother.

There was a particular incident only a few months after my marriage. Christmas was coming and it was my wish to visit the Church on Christmas day. So, after finishing my daily chores, I decided to visit the Church and did so. When I got back home, I could sense some unpleasantness in my in-laws; they were upset with me. They protested, saying that I must stop visiting the Church now that I am married into a Brahmin family. I should only follow Hinduism. We argued for some time, and then there was a sudden sense of realization in me: "What am I doing? Why am I reacting to this situation? God or Family? Church or No Church? I married a man whom I love. That is it. When it comes to God, first is my family, then God."

By 20, I became a mother to a son. It was then that I began pondering and questioning my beliefs and the realities of life. "What am I going to teach my son?" What if my son goes to my in-laws and they say, "Don't go to church." and then my child comes to me and I say, "Don't go to the temple." Who would be the victim here? My child. All I wanted to do was instill the right values in my children, so I decided not to fight my situation and gratefully accepted Hinduism as a way of life. Luckily, I could accept my situation due to my upbringing and my faith in My Almighty (whomever it may be). So I started practicing Hinduism regularly even though mechanically. We had a small temple in our house with idols of all sorts of Gods and Goddesses; you name it, it was there (Ganesha, Maha Kali, Hanuman, Krishna).

There was this one instance when my mother-in-law was not well. As a result, I was supposed to light the diya (candle) on her behalf in the temple. At first, I was excited that "I" get to light the diya today. However, when I entered the temple, I was literally scared to see the faces of the idols and quickly lit the diya and rushed out of the room. The moment I stepped out of the temple, the first thought that came to me was, "How can I worship a God I am afraid to even look at?" But my heart replied, "I have no right to pass such judgments or speak against any religion. If I really want to know why this is a Ganesh or why this looks like a monkey or an elephant, there is a reason behind it. There is a history behind it which I need to know. I must know about this religion if I am working so hard for it."

Every Brahmin family has one senior *pundit* (religious scholar) who performs all the Hindu rituals. The pundit of our family has a son who completed his *acharya*, the highest degree of Brahmin. So I asked him, "I really want to know about your religion. Could you educate me on this subject?" My thought was to create the right religious environment in our home. He agreed and taught me all about the Hindu religion explaining the Bhagavad Gita, the Shiv Puran, Devi Bhagavatam – all those religious books where the gods reveal exactly what they are, what Shakti (power) is, what the symbols mean. I learned and started following all the Hindu rituals diligently.

Later we shifted from Nagaland to Arunachal due to my husband's business commitments. By then, I was already a mother of three children, a son and two daughters. One fine afternoon, we decided to go for a family picnic at the riverside. While taking a stroll, I found a beautiful Shiv Linga (the holy stone of Lord Shiva), which I picked up and brought home to place in my temple along with all the other idols. I showed it to one of the pundit, who was impressed because the stone had all the features projecting Lord Shiva. It was jet black in color and had "Jatta," "Trishul" and "Om" engraved on it. The pundit asked me to worship this particular Shiv Linga and told me that this particular Shiv Linga was a Jagrit stone (awakened stone). We got the parthav [shivling] puja done and placed it at home in my temple.

I became a true Brahmin. My routine was to get up at 4 o'clock in the morning and I would start by washing all the utensils that I used at the temple and giving a bath to the Linga with milk and curd, then offering ghee and mustard oil for lighting the diya (candle). I used to wear a rudraksh necklace and would jaap (chant) for hours with the same necklace. Fasting on Monday was a must. This went on for almost six years. However, somewhere deep inside me, I was still in search of something. I wasn't aware what exactly it was, but I kept on searching and searching.

I do remember getting fed up and saying, "What is this? You are a stone. I have been sitting here for the past six years trying to get answers and I'm not getting them. The book which you have written is thousands of years old and hence cannot be applied at present. I have a problem today. How do I resolve it? I need a human – a human who can scold me, who can guide me, who can hold my hand and walk with me. I need someone." I said, "You are not giving me anything that I'm looking for. I have been sincere from the bottom of my heart and kept trying to connect with you – and I can't. I'm sorry, I've crossed my limit." That day, I think I must have cried for almost an hour, finally falling asleep in my temple.

Since a very young age, I have wondered about life, how one should live it, how one should think about it. I shared a good relationship with many of the priests in the nearby temples, even though they were often much older than me. I liked to sit with them and gain knowledge and wisdom about life. It so happened, a very renowned Rishi (seer, saint) from Haridwar visited. He preferred to walk as a means of transport rather than use vehicles. He never consumed salt in his food. He came with two or three pundits to my house and I took him to my temple. He looked at the temple and he was very happy to see the way I had kept everything so nicely and he told me, "*Mataji* (mother), you have made this a beautiful temple. Everything is so beautiful."

Then suddenly he became furious! He looked at me and said, "Do you think the food you have offered to the God is going to be eaten?" I said, "What he gives me is what I have offered."

He looked at me and he said, "Bang your head on this stone. You will bleed. You will die. But it will not eat what you have offered." I was taken aback! I was stunned! I wondered what was happening and why he was talking to me this way! I thought a Rishi of that caliber would have more humility and etiquette. Then he screamed at me and said, "This is not what you're supposed to do!" so I said, "What am I supposed to do?" and he said, "Rise above." I said, "How?" He said, "Stop doing all this. Go beyond it. What you're doing is wasting your time." I was very disappointed and upset. I continued to be upset for a month or more after he left. This, however, was part of what I now think of as my journey from religion to spirituality.

Kim: How did you become interested in meditation with Sahaj Marg?

My youngest sister faced a lot of problems as a child. She was always a very sensitive child, able to see things which other humans could not see, including paranormal activities and supernatural beings like spirits. She was only three years old when my father passed away. I remember her telling me, "I can see Papa and he's calling me, waving." It seemed, as part of the condition, her health was deteriorating and she was often sick. My mother looked for help, worried about my sister's health and well-being. She went to the church. She went to the temple. She went to the mosque. She did everything possible for her daughter, looking for whomever could help her, but nothing seemed to help. So I decided to bring her to Arunachal to stay with me for a while. I hoped we could find a solution for her problem, or at least find some way to help.

My sister was 18 or 19 years old when she came to stay with me in Arunachal Pradesh. I was given advice by a gentleman in Itanagar who said, "The problem is inside and you're looking outside. You have to find a system to help internally, not externally." He mentioned a man who might be able to help in Arunachal so, the next day, I made an appointment and went to see him. This is how Sahaj Marg entered my family. It was through my sister.

Mr. Xxx explained to me about the system and suggested that the problems my sister was facing were internal and related to impressions, most likely from the past. As a prefect, he suggested a session each day for three days with monitoring. He felt sure he could help her. My goal was that she should get well. So my sister started with meditation. She was quite regular with her practice. However, after a month or two, she would sit down to meditate and see an old man sitting there and telling her not to do this. I was confused. What to do? When I reported this to the prefect, he said, "Don't worry. Maybe there's something which needs to come out. Things are happening."

She kept doing the meditation but I was not involved. I really had no idea what the system was all about. I continued to be regular with my puja (worship), as before. The prefect would often offer and ask me, "Why don't you start meditating?" and I would say, "No, I'm very happy with what I'm doing. I'm worshipping all the *Devi-Devtas* (Goddesses, Gods) and I'm very, very happy with it."

Two months or so after my sister entered Sahaj Marg, I was still worried about her. I was sitting in the office when suddenly I thought, "Why not speak to that old man, the Master?" I thought, "What harm is there if I speak to him and take my sister?" So I called up the prefect and said, "I would like to meet your Master." He was a very smart prefect. He said, "Well, I can take you but what is the point of just going like that? Why don't you also start so that you will have something to talk to him about?" I said, "I want to go and meet your Master and request him to make my sister all right. If that is what it takes, then I don't mind starting." So he said okay. He said, "I am going to come tomorrow. I'm going to be there by 8 o'clock." I loved my sister so much that I was willing to do anything for her. So he came at 8 o'clock in the morning and he explained what to do and how to do it. I sat down and I just put up a prayer saying, "Here I am. I'm sitting down. I know nothing about the system, but I have faith that God is within me. So let me sit." That very first sitting was the turning point of my life.

The very first sitting, I could literally hear my heart beat. After nearly 20 minutes of the sitting, I could hear it go like "thup-thup-thup-thup." In my meditation, I'm talking to myself, "Oh my God! This is what I have been looking for so many years! You are inside me and I'm like a stupid person, looking outside!" After the sitting finished, I started crying. The prefect just looked at me and said, "It happens." I said, "What do you mean, "It happens?" He said, "After the sitting, usually a lot of people feel that." I said, "You know what? These tears are out of joy. These tears are not out of sadness. These tears are not out of cleaning. There is so much joy in my heart that I have found what I was looking for."

I took my three sittings and I entered a new life. I have not looked back. I was never a person who liked reading literature so I was happy when the prefect told me, "Just do your cleaning and meditation and that's it." He put no pressure on me regarding any other features of the system like constant remembrance, nine o'clock prayer, volunteer work, nothing! He said, "Do your cleaning, do your meditation, just these two things." I followed religiously. He said, "In three months' time, you will see the difference." And I did start feeling a lot of things internally. I would not say I had a vision, but there were a lot of internal palpitations, vibrations – at certain points, my whole body shaking; so many things. I was enjoying it. I was literally enjoying it. I said, "Wow! This is a good thing."

And then slowly, slowly, at the back of my mind, the thoughts would crop up that I still have a temple in my house and I was meditating in the temple. I put up a prayer to Master saying, "I will not listen to anybody but you. I will only listen to you. I will follow you as per your command, as per your order." I said, "I have been doing this *puja* ritual for the past six years now and I cannot just pick up and throw away all the idols because then I will have guilt in me. I don't want to have guilt. So, the day you feel that I am ready, I will not think twice. I will pick up everything and do whatsoever is needed." So I continued with the idol worship and rituals along with Sahaj Marg practice. After not even a year, one fine day early in the morning, when I was meditating in my temple, I heard a clear voice: "Enough. You can pick it up." It was such a clear voice that I immediately got up and picked up everything. All the photographs made out of silver, I picked up and distributed to all the small temples. The holy stone (*Shiva ling*) was *visarjit* (let go in the water) in the river. While doing the ritual of *visarjan*, I prayed, "Whoever gets this *Shiva ling*, let there be enlightenment in his life."

That was my stepping-stone to spirituality; it was. Maybe it was something related to my past that I had to follow three religions – Christian, Jewish, Hindu – but only through Him, I could reach Sahaj Marg. Babuji Maharaj said it clearly – that where religion ends, spirituality begins. At that point, I became very, very regular with my *sadhana* (meditation practice).

Kim: How did you know this was the right path to follow?

Several things happened to prove to me that this was the right path. For example, it had been a year since I joined the Mission and I did not have a single photograph of my Master. There was a brother from the Mission who worked for Doordarshan (an Indian national television station) and was shifting to Delhi from Arunachal. He had an old photograph of Master on his wall and his wife continuously told him, "Pack this. Pack this." but he never did. One day, when I went to his house, I said, "I have been meditating for almost a year but I don't have Master's photo." He gave me his, saying, "Maybe this was for you." I still have that photograph. It's almost faded now, but I still keep it in my meditation room in Arunachal Pradesh.

A year or two later, I was told that my daughter, who was at boarding school in Mussoorie, may have the chicken pox. I was asked to go to Mussoorie to fetch her from the hostel but somewhere deep inside me, I questioned this plan, thinking, "She needs to see a doctor but it will take some time for me to get there to help her." I thought, "I'll just tell my sister-in-law, who is nearby. She can pick her up and take her to the doctor." Meanwhile, Master was in Calcutta. I decided to go to Calcutta and be with Him for two days, then proceed to Mussoorie.

When I went to Calcutta, the prefect told me, "Sister, be ready." I said, "Be ready? For what?" I couldn't connect. Then I realized he meant that Master wanted to make me a prefect! I was not told, no hint, nothing. I said, "Please wait. I am not prepared. Give me one more year. I have just done my *sadhana* (spiritual practice) for two years and I feel I need to evolve more before I take up this responsibility." He looked at me and he said, "No. You are prepared for it." I had no time to think. My heart was also trying to speak to me: "If you are saying no, why are you here?" I could hear it speaking to me! Then I saw Master coming out of his bedroom, walking towards me, and my heart is saying again, "Then why are you here? Why are you practicing so much?" Then the fourth question came, when Master asked me, "Are you ready for the *puja*?" and I just looked at him. I said yes, because I got all my answers. If I don't believe in the system, then why am I here? I should've been somewhere else (probably with my daughter).

There were around nine or ten of us there who were being prepared to become prefects. I was sitting right in front of Master when he looked at me and asked, "When do you want to go?" So I told Master, "My daughter is not well. They're suspecting chicken pox or something like that. Master, I need to be there in two days." For a second, he looked away and then he looked back at me and said, "I don't think at this time she should be having chicken pox." That's it. He was telling me I didn't need to worry about it. (As it turns out, indeed, it was a small skin infection.)

Usually, when preparing an abhyasi to become a prefect, quite a few sittings are given. I was given just one sitting, one beautiful sitting. I was totally knocked out. After that I was not aware of anything, be it my slippers or clothes. I was totally in a different condition for several days. It changed my life.

Previously, I had never been an outgoing person. I was a business lady and simultaneously took care of my house. My only friend was my husband. That was enough. Business time was just a business. My meditation time was just my meditation time. I was not so social and preferred to be in silence. I preferred spending time at home in private.

After Master made me a prefect, I went out and spoke my heart out about Sahaj Marg by knocking on doors. Door-to-door in Dehradun, whomever I knew, I said, "Try. Do it. It's so beautiful. It'll change your life completely. What you see is not reality." Whatever little I knew at that time, I shared, going house to house.

This made my father-in-law furious and he would scream at me, "You are not taking care of your kids and you're going and preaching about Sahaj Marg." I thought, "Let me get scolded, fine, but let me do my part. I should not miss out on this moment that has been given to me. I have been made a prefect, so my duty is to do as much as I can. I'm supposed to do it." And I did it. We started having Wednesday satsangh in the Dehradun house because we were quite a bunch of new abhyasis. Today, I am very happy whenever I visit Dehradun; they're all regular abhyasis. That is how my prefect journey started.

Kim: Do you have any special experiences or memories to share?

Sahaj Marg is a journey filled with experiences. I still remember my experience when I shifted to my new house in Gurgaon. My husband had business in Arunachal Pradesh and I was there alone. However, one evening, I felt as if somebody was there with me. I was scared. I felt as if someone was lying down next to me and breathing. When I opened my eyes to look, there was nobody around. I put out the thought, "I am Lalaji's abhyasi." I had read in a book where Lalaji says, "If you're scared of anything, just think that you are Lalaji's abhyasi." At one point, I thought, "Why are you so scared? And if you are, why don't you call your relatives?" I had people nearby; I could've just called – but then my heart was saying, "If you have faith in your Master, he says that he is going to take care of you every moment; this is the time to check your faith." I said, "Fine, if he wants me to die, I'll die. If he wants me to go through this, I will face it. I will not call anybody." I became set in that decision. I thought, "If I have to die, if somebody has to come and do something here, let it happen." In this way, one night passed. On Saturday, the same thing happened again; I felt something there. Sunday came and I went to the ashram, returning around two o'clock. A new abhyasi wanted me to go and have lunch, so I went out again until around four o'clock. That night was somehow okay.

The next morning, however, my maid comes and tells me, "Do you know that just above your house an old lady committed suicide?" I said, "What?" She said, "Yes, right above your bedroom. She jumped from there and died." I said, "Oh my God. I didn't know anything about this." She asked me, "Where were you?" and I explained I had been out most of the day on Sunday. She told me about the police coming, that they had taken the body, and things like that.

I didn't know who to call or where to go. I was crying. I just put up a prayer and said, "I need a sitting. Master, please connect with me." You wouldn't believe it! I didn't call. I just put up a prayer. In just five minutes, I got a call from a prefect. He said, "Yes. What happened?" I said, "I need a sitting. I'm in a real bad state. I need a sitting." He said, "I'm coming." During my sitting, I could feel a fountain flowing from my heart. It did not stop until the sitting was over. What a sitting it was! I was left with absolutely no fear, no impression. Absolutely, I was back to normal in just 30 minutes. I really saluted Master on the system. I said, "Master, what a beautiful system this is."

Another experience that I would like to share is when Master invited me to Satkhol, the Himalayan Ashram. I had never heard of it. When he invited me, I wondered where it was but said okay and went. It was high in the Himalayas in the month of September or October, pretty cold! This was another turning point to know what Sahaj Marg is all about.

In the middle of the night, around 1:00-1:30 am., I heard a clear voice, "Joshna!" That's it. I got up and looked around but everybody was sleeping. I got really scared and thought, "What is this? From where did I hear my name?" In the middle of the night, I heard a voice, just my name, just once, and it was like a command, like an army officer calling your name out – "Joshna!" That's it. Not even, "Get up." But I thought, "What is the point of doing my meditation now? It's the middle of the night." So I tried to sleep but I just couldn't. I tried for 20 minutes, turning, twisting, but I just couldn't sleep. Finally, I said, "Let me get up, sit and try and meditate." It was cold so I totally wrapped myself with a blanket and sat.

I sat and closed my eyes and "Oh my God!" There was a burning sensation which started right from my toenails! I was burning. It started coming up gradually. I could even feel the burning sensation inside my eyeballs. I understood something special was happening. At one point, I wanted to vomit and I thought, "If I vomit, all my clothes in this cold will become messy." My mind was trying to tell me, "If you vomit, you've had it." But somewhere my heart was saying, "Vomit." I literally opened my mouth. I said, "Let it get messed up. It's okay. Maybe this is what is needed." So I vomited. I could feel something, all coming out – but nothing was there. Nothing actually came out, but I could feel it had [all been expelled]. After [awhile], slowly, slowly, it subsided completely and I just went off to sleep. I will never forget this experience and have written about it in my diary. This was well beyond cleaning. It was literally like I could feel each and every cell of my body purified. It was an amazing experience that lasted 25-30 minutes.

Kim: Did you feel you had to give anything up or was there anything that was difficult for you when starting the practice?

I came for the first bhandara in Chennai in the year 2002. I just put up a very subtle thought, "I wish I could become vegetarian." I knew my biggest weakness was non-veg food. I could sacrifice everything but this was something for which I was totally dependent on Master because, when it comes to food habits, we as a family were all non-vegetarian. Every meal was non-veg. But somewhere I read that, if you want to grow spiritually, anything which is gross should not be taken in. Spirituality is very subtle and, to absorb it, one has to become sensitive. To develop sensitivity in order to experience the subtleness of spirituality, one needs to have a pure vegetarian diet.

After the bhandara, when I went back to Dehradun, my husband told me, "Enough of vegetarian food. Now cook non-veg." I said, "Okay." So he bought some mutton and chicken and I cooked everything. I laid out the table and everybody was sitting, including my sister-in-law, who is a vegetarian (I cooked veg food for her). I sat down and picked up a bowl of meat, planning to serve myself." You wouldn't believe it! When I picked up the bowl and was just about to put it on my plate, I could hear a voice saying, "Don't have it." I got scared. I looked around. I thought, "Who's talking to me?" I didn't know I was so sensitive. I was such a stupid person. I never knew what the word 'sensitivity' was. I thought, "What is this? Where is it coming from?" So I put down the bowl, scared, then served myself some dal and vegetables. My husband asked me, "What's wrong with you? Not in a good mood? How come you're not eating this?" Again, I picked up the bowl of mutton and heard the same voice. Again, I put it back. The third time I picked up the bowl and put it back, I said, "No." Since that day, I have not eaten meat (non-veg). It was only Master who could take out such deep-rooted inner desire to eat non-veg food. I would not have done it on my own. It was only His grace that made me do it. That was a shocking thing for my family, especially my husband. I still cook non-veg for my family. I only pray to Master, make them so satisfied [with veg] that they don't even look at it [non-veg] again. This is only what I can do for them. I can't say, "Stop eating." But I'm seeing a lot of changes now in my family.

Kim: I wonder if you have any other interesting stories to share?

An unfortunate incident took place in my maternal family which turned out to be a spiritual experience for me. I lost my brother in the year 2008. During this incident, my mother was in the U.S.A. with both my sisters who had married and settled there. I was in Gurgaon when I was informed that he (my brother) had died in his sleep. I left immediately for Dimapur, Nagaland and asked his wife to keep his body until I arrived. We had to bury him with all the rituals of Christianity. The church members and the priest kept his body the whole night and were singing devotional songs. I arrived quite late at night, around 11.30 pm. When I saw the dead body of my brother, there were tears in my eyes but my heart was observing everything around me. His face looked peaceful. He looked very handsome in the black suit. [But] I could feel an inner awakening inside me. A very strange thing happened. I could see and feel a very different picture from that of the people crying and sitting around the dead body. I felt people cry of their own guilt, not for the person who had left the world.

Sitting in front of my brother's dead body, I talked about Sahaj Marg to the church members until 4 a.m., and then I went to my room and sat down for my cleaning. I could see (through my inner vision) and feel strong, dark, opaque shadows in front of me. They were trying to stop me from doing my cleaning. I kept putting my force to continue my cleaning process but a point came when it came so close to me, I thought it was going to attack me. I got scared but then, that very moment, I had the magical thought, "I am the disciple of Lalaji." I could feel a sense of relief.

The same morning, around 7.30 a.m., I sat for my meditation. It was very deep and engrossing. Suddenly I heard a voice in my meditation saying, "*Kuch chakkar hai*" (something is not right). Instantly I felt that my brother's death was not natural. I thought of sending his body for post mortem but as I continued meditating, I remembered Master's saying that "everything is an excuse," meaning that everyone has to die and will die; the reason is just "an excuse." I dropped the post mortem plan and we buried my Brother's body with all the rituals. Master revealed to me the reality of my brother's death eight months later. There had been foul play. The next morning I clearly remember as a special experience. I sat for my meditation and put up a prayer to Master that I wanted to feel my brother's presence. Three times, the bed on which I was meditating was moved and lifted, but this time I was not scared. I said, "that's it" and it stopped; that was enough for me.

These experiences have made my heart more open. I have felt my evolution as a spiritual person. [I believe] as long as we live, at least try your best to do your part so that you have no regrets. Forgive everyone and have no expectations if you want to reach your goal. My faith has become stronger and stronger. Anytime I wanted any answer from Master, I could just sit and meditate and he would just reply in one word or in one sentence. I have gone through a lot in life but I survived every challenge because I kept holding him tight. I always prayed to Master, saying, "I'm totally dependent on you. You have to hold my hand and show me the direction." Every step of my life he has shown me a direction; I never took decisions on my own. Till today I don't take decisions; I put up a prayer and I leave it to him. I have so many experiences that I don't even remember. There is absolutely no end to miracles.

Kim: I wonder if you could talk a little more about family life and the practice? I think it's interesting to get a mother's point of view.

Sahaj Marg taught me that parenting is an art, not a duty. When it comes to parenting, I have never forced my children to do anything. Both the daughters went to boarding school when one was in fifth grade and the other fourth grade. I told them, "Baby, you can't expect Mama to be there… When in need of anything, put up a prayer to Master because he can reach you very fast. He can solve your problem. You just have to call him. Have faith. You need someone who can guide you and help you before Mama is with you." This is how the prayer was introduced to my children.

My daughter shared a beautiful experience of how prayer helped her. She was in seventh grade and her final exams were on and somebody stole her notebook. She was crying when she called me up to ask, "Mama, now how do I study? How can I appear for the exam?" She was crying and crying. She must've been praying to Master in her own way. She got an idea and stuck up a letter saying, "Whoever has taken my notebook, kindly put it back where you picked it up from. I will not tell anybody." Two days before her exam, she got the notebook back. She called and told me, "Mama, that book was lying in the same drawer where I left it." I told her, "Do you realize now how Master helps you? Don't you think this is a better way to communicate? Mom can make mistakes but Master cannot make mistakes." She said, "Yes, Mama."

My son voluntarily started his meditation. My elder daughter also started voluntarily but my youngest daughter told me, "Mom, I am not going to randomly just take a sitting. I want to be very serious; I don't want to take it lightly. So I will not start until and unless my heart says." I was just putting up a prayer to Master. I said, "Master, please take care of her. I don't know what to do." I was in Chennai and it was my younger daughter's birthday. We had gone to Master's residence, Gayatri, to meet him. We were waiting and suddenly Brother Xxx comes out and says, "Whose birthday is it today?" My daughter said, "Today is my birthday." "Oh, you wanted a sitting? Come, come, come." My daughter looked at me and said, "Mom, I'm not going to take sitting." I told her, "Okay. You sit outside and I will go in." She said, "No, no, no. I also want to come in." I said, "It's up to you." She said, "It's my birthday and I want to meet Master. When we entered Gayatri, Master asked her to sit in front of him and started the satsangh. After the sitting Master looked at her and said, "You should have taken sitting after [waiting] two years. I gave to you early." She felt so bad. She asked me, "Was I not prepared?" I said, "No, baby. He's done two years' work in this first sitting." She expresses all her feelings and emotions to Master without any fear or guilt. Her blind faith in Master reflects her strong connection with Him. I can say all this today because she has openly expressed her wish to get married to the boy Master selects for her. This gives me a sense of satisfaction and contentment that I have done my part as a parent. I would also like to mention that the roots of the students of Omega school [run by the Mission] are very strong. The values are strong and their concept of life is very clear. There is no confusion.

I have always tried to be a living example to my children. I have never preached. I have always told my husband, "Try to become. Don't preach and do not try to impress your children with money." I see most fathers try to impress their children by fulfilling their materialistic desires, perhaps because they want to cover up their guilt of not spending much time with their kids. So I told my husband, "Your children need you and you have to be a living example."

One beautiful thing that Master keeps saying is, "Work on yourself. Forget about what is happening around you. You have to reach a level higher than them so that automatically, once you start evolving and reach certain vibratory levels, they will automatically start getting attracted towards you." I have realized this is happening. I have seen the moment I have been pushed up one level. Suddenly I'm seeing a change in my children. I'm seeing a change in my husband, too.

There's a saying, 'Before a rocket takes off, initially you need a lot of pressure.' So I have put so much of my effort – talking, guiding and molding – just to give them a base. One thing I have understood in the past five years is that I don't have any expectations from my children. I mean that, if you have groomed them in the right way and given them unconditional love, they will respond the right way, as and when nature wants them to respond. Otherwise, our thoughts or expectations of them can become barriers to their progress.

The second thing is that my duty is to give them a spiritual environment. That is my duty. How they grow from that is [according to] their effort and *samskara*. I have to be a living example to my children so that they look upon me as a guide. I always tell my children, "You all have chosen me. I have not chosen you." You chose me as your mother while you were in the soul condition. There was some connection between us. You chose to come down because you knew that this mother would help you to achieve your goals. When you were in that soul condition, you had this thought. Now just because you have come down in the physical form you have lost that contact. I am reminding you that you have come for a higher purpose."

Every time I could revert them back to a better condition and they could again connect and become regular with their meditation and things like that.

I have seen that, as you grow spiritually, your family also grows. I am seeing this right in front of my eyes. You attract people of the same level. If you have a problem with your marriage, your surroundings will all be that. If you are a very aggressive person, you will only attract those people. Now, as I am going ahead in my spiritual journey, I'm seeing better things. When I'm seeing better things, I automatically see that unwanted things are just shedding off without my putting any effort. It's beautifully falling off. I can just observe and see how nature is working. Very silently, I've been observing it.

Kim: Could you speak a little bit about balance and surrender? What do those ideas mean to you?

When I see all these things, I think, "Why do we humans have to put our mind to solve a problem? Let him handle it." To reach this stage of realization, one has to have blind faith and inculcate feelings of total surrender in Him. Why put your mind into something where you don't belong? Just leave it.

Surrender as a practice takes a lot of time. It can only happen through practice. It cannot happen without practice. If you have 99.9% faith, 0.1% of doubt can pull you down badly. Every day, every moment, my motive in life is that I don't want to make any mistakes that will hamper my smooth journey of spiritual evolution. I live every day with that principle. I get up with that thought every morning. I want to pay off all my debts, if any, before I die because I don't intend to come back to pay the debtors in my next life. Master has given me enough and has opened my heart to help others with no expectations. I have learnt that you cannot help anybody, you cannot give to anybody and you cannot teach anybody, unless and until your heart is wide open. When your heart is open, he works.

Master has always taught us that both spiritual and material life need to be balanced. But how? It's like a weighing scale. At one point of time, the balance falls on one side but is too much. You need to balance it up again. You try to put something on the other side… so you have to fall from both sides to balance it permanently. I was too spiritual at one point in time. When I became too spiritual, I saw a lot of things being neglected but it was the need of the hour for me to grow. So I was put in that condition, giving more and investing more time in meditation to become sensitive enough to know what material life can teach me. Then it pushed me back and made me fall down on the other side. I realized I didn't need so much!" So I said, "No, no, no. Now I know my limit. I can survive with this much." So you start slowly, slowly balancing and then suddenly you know exactly where you need to balance 50:50.

When you know how to balance 50:50, you become a balanced wife, a balanced mother, a balanced daughter and ultimately a balanced human being. You become perfect in everything you do in your life. Believe me. I have never constructed or designed a house. Again, it was a challenge for me and from within me. Master had told me once that, "Whatever you do, you will perfect it." It was a complete thing when I constructed my house. In my meditation, I would see a vision and I would go and tell them to do exactly that. Everything turned out as per the need. No space was wasted. It was balanced; not less, not more. Everything was planned so that I am able to do things myself in old age. Another teaching of Sahaj Marg that I learnt through my experience was - you live for the present, but you can see the future.

Kim: How important is faith? Is faith more important than discipline?

One thing I know is that, when you are put in one level, you need to pass that level. Until and unless you pass that level, he will not give you another level because he doesn't want his child to fall again and again rise up. So, whatever the situation that is given to us, believe me, if you practice and adapt it with faith and sincerity, it works wonders.

Maybe you don't have faith initially – but, with practice, you develop discipline in your life. In Sahaj Marg, discipline is getting up on time, doing your meditation at a fixed time every morning, cleaning on time and always being in his remembrance. It may feel artificial at first, but start to make it real. One thing I've seen is that, as you keep practicing Sahaj Marg with sincerity, you become in tune with nature. Even animals and plants respond to your love and affection. So when this system slowly, slowly, without you knowing, becomes a part of you, the obedience starts. When the obedience starts, you're willing to practice it with sincerity. Once the momentum builds up, the love for the system develops. One feels incomplete without the system and starts enjoying the process of meditation. This is the third stage of meditation. Master says, "It should become your lifestyle."

Love can only come if you practice with discipline, then obedience, then love, then faith and then blind faith. Not before that! It's a long journey but it can be very short if you practice sincerely from the initial stage. If you're regular with your meditation for six months, believe me, nothing can stop you from this journey.

Kim: You seem to have had a lot of interesting experiences relating to spirituality and the spirit world. Have you any more to share with us?

I have another story in which Master gave me an opportunity to handle another [death] situation, but in a more refined manner. It was the death of my father-in-law. He was 96 years old when he died. While he was living, I tried my best to convince him to join meditation but he was never interested. Moreover, he used to tell me not to neglect my family for such spiritual practices.

He felt spirituality is to be adopted in the later stages of life, when you become old and free of all responsibilities.

When we were informed of the death of my father-in-law, I left home and reached their house as soon as I could. When I arrived, I was disappointed to see the way his dead body was kept, to my eyes, untidy and shabby. I always believed that when a man dies his body should be respected and given a grand exit. Being Christian, we are very particular about getting flower bouquets and so on. I left immediately for the market and purchased bunches of flowers, perfume, *dhoop* (incense) and white sheets of cloth for the body. I returned and changed the sheet of the mattress on which the body was kept, covered the body with another white sheet, sprinkled perfume, lit the dhoop and decorated flowers in the entire room. The room became so beautiful.

Even though it was cold during the month of December, most in Hindu religion don't want to keep the dead body at home. They want to discard it as soon as possible. My aunt was saying, "No, no, no, we should cremate the body," wanting to call the priest but I told them, "You will not do it because his son is not here. Two sons are not here. I want them to see him for the last time." I offered to take care of him all night. "Don't worry about it. I will not put pressure on you people, but I will make sure that both the sons see their father for the last time." They got a little upset and left.

By midnight, I was all alone with the dead body and was reading the book My Master (Rajagopalachari, 1989). In that, it was written that a prefect had been given the power to work on a dead body. As long as the body is not cremated, the prefect can work on it. I didn't know that. I thought, "Why this page at this moment?" and thought I must try. So I just closed my eyes and put up a prayer to Master. I saw my father-in-law sitting down in front of me. When I opened my eyes, I saw the dead body. I closed my eyes and again he's sitting! Then I started pinching myself; maybe after midnight I am sleepy. When I open my eyes, he's lying there as a dead body and when I close my eyes, he's sitting. So I thought, "Then let me give him a sitting." You won't believe it! Throughout the night, he was taking an individual sitting from me. The spiritual work went on and on till 3 a.m. in the morning. I was just thinking, "When you were alive, I wanted you to join meditation. I always wanted to give you a sitting. And now, after you have left your physical form, you are taking a sitting."

Around 3 a.m., my husband started calling and the whole family came and sat in front of the body. I thought, "It's okay, fine. The work is done and that's what matters to me. I don't need to prove anything to anybody." I only have to ask myself as a prefect, "Have I done my work well or not?"

The next experience I would like to share is one I cherish because it made me realize that one can be in strong spiritual contact without physically being present. For Master's birthday gathering or celebration, called a *bhandara*, we all start our preparations well in advance. The excitement and craving to be in bhandara makes us restless and we cannot wait to be there. A week before Master's birthday bhandara, Master had visited Siliguri to inaugurate an ashram. When I saw him there, he looked at me and asked, "How are you feeling?" I replied, "I am good, Master." Three days later, I had a severe backache due to a chronic urinary tract infection. The pain was unbearable and I fainted, was airlifted out and taken to the hospital. Master's birthday bhandara was nearing so I told the doctor I didn't want to get admitted to hospital. The doctor said, "You still have some days before bhandara. Let us admit you and then we will see." I was admitted in the hospital with reports showing kidney abscess but was adamant I wanted to attend the bhandara.

My son and older daughter left for the bhandara. My daughter was very upset and wanted to meet Master to update him on my health condition. She had an opportunity at a book launch.

There was a long queue to purchase the book as Master was handing it over himself. She purchased the book and managed to convey my health condition to Master. Master said, "Don't worry, she will be fine. I will pray for her."

Here in the hospital, I settled down with the thought of not being able to attend the bhandara. Master, however, gave me an opportunity to be in a beautiful condition, an experience of a lifetime. I was very calm, not aware of my physical condition or environment. This condition remained for three days. I was in a state of permanent meditation, unaware of any pain and removed from happenings around me.

I very strongly feel that, if you are connected from the heart with Master, it becomes very easy for Him to work. You don't need to be around Him physically to experience his grace; it flows everywhere. You just have to make your heart open and capable so that it becomes receptive.

Kim: How do you know you are doing well and making progress?

I'm not answerable to anyone but to my Master. I don't want to disappoint Master. I want him always to be proud of me. When I stand in front of him, I want to see him happy. That is my goal. I want to see a smile on his face, "Yes, my child. At least I have some hope in you that you're doing something good." I always try to work on myself so much before I go to him. If he gives me something, I'm going to go back home and work on myself so much that when I go and meet him again he'll push me on to the next higher level. That is the craving I have. I crave to prove myself silently to my Master without anybody being aware of it, without talking, with just eye contact with Him. That is the level of commitment I have toward him.

I am so grateful to my Master for holding my hand and guiding me to the right path with so much love. I joined Sahaj Marg with a ray of hope – to grow in spirituality – but He has converted my hope into a strong belief of reaching the ultimate goal, Complete Oneness with Him.

Sahaj Marg is an experience in itself. Thank you.

Chapter 3

The Subtle Divine Within

Pascale

French, female, early 60's, eye therapist

Preface: I met Pascale on my third trip to Chennai (formerly Madras). I was staying at a friend's guest house, cooking meals for him for fun, and she was invited for lunch. A strikingly pretty blonde woman, active and graceful in middle age, I am impressed with her lively personality and her true interest in those around her. I feel a sisterly connection even though we both fumble with language, me with no French and she uncomfortable in English. Over fresh beet salad, I learned that she and her husband do quantic therapy (see references and book one of this series where Gilles, Pascale's husband, talks about their work in some detail).

Pascale has served 35 years as a meditation trainer and preceptor (see glossary). She gives me a 1:1 sitting and I feel at peace, as though a burden has lifted off my heart. We make an appointment and agree to do the interview at our friend's house so our friend can translate when needed. Although we are often speaking through the translator, Pascale speaks wonderfully about the heart and the need to follow one's heart as a main life principle, especially in our spiritual lives. She gives down-to-earth yet moving explanations of 'constant remembrance' and 'surrender.' She explains how she approaches and integrates those concepts in a very real way within her daily life, moment to moment. I hope you will enjoy meeting this lovely lady and appreciate her sharing and advice.

Kim: Could you please introduce yourself, telling about your background and about how you became interested in spirituality?

My name is Pascale. I have been interested in spirituality since birth and met Sahaj Marg through my mother, who meditated once with Babuji in Paris. I was looking to do yoga and for a spiritual path. My mother said there was a very good group in Toulon in the south of France and gave me the address. I was 28 years old when I took my first sitting.

Kim: There was almost nobody in Europe at that point, right?

There were very few but Toulon was the second biggest center in France after Nice. There were about twenty people. So I began. At the time, I was in the process of getting divorced and I was raising two young children by myself, so I could not continue because of the hours of the meditation group. It was very difficult as a single parent. At the time, it wasn't structured as it is now. It was just group meditations in the morning and sittings. There weren't the personal practices and it was less structured than it is now.

Kim: Is that because they had not worked out the method yet? Or was it just evolving?

No, it was because the preceptor was doing his own method. They called it the "Purified Method." It was very light. He knew Babuji. All the preceptors were nominated by Babuji.

Kim: You were a single parent and you were starting the practice?

I had to stop Sahaj Marg for a while and went to look for spirituality elsewhere. I tried many different paths, many; at least ten. I would stay six months and my heart would say, "No, this is not right." I did this ten times and one day my heart told me, "But you remember you started a meditation on the heart? You have to return."

Kim: Ah! So you listened to your heart?

Yes. Thank you for recognizing that! So I looked to re-start meditation. I began with Babuji and my heart told me to return to Sahaj Marg, so I re-started Sahaj Marg in 1982. During September of 1982, Babuji came to France and was in Paris but, again, I couldn't go because I had small children and school was starting. I had not seized the importance of the occasion. When all the abhyasis returned from Paris, I understood what I had missed. So I promised myself I would go to India the following summer to see him.

Kim: That's a big commitment!

He died the following April. I didn't know right away that he had died. He came to me in my dreams three days after his death. He came to me and sat at the edge of my bed. He had the divine light around his head and his eyes had the same divine halo that surrounded me. I will never forget the light.

I was on a cloud for three days. Then I heard that he was dead.

Kim: So you knew it was him?

I had done the [introductory] sittings in 1977 and started again in 1982. I was meditating with him and saw photos. My first Master was Babuji.

The day he died, I had an experience while I was working. I had a patient in front of me. I was on the third floor and there was a window behind me. All of a sudden, I felt something entering my back that went straight into my heart. I looked back to see what it was and there was no one there. I found out later that this was the day he died. I truly felt that he had put light into my heart.

Kim: Wow! And have you been coming to India ever since?

Chariji came to Toulon in 1985; then I decided to come to India, but because Babuji had died, I didn't know where to go. Just before leaving, I met a friend (also a preceptor abhyasi) in the street. He said, "I've been looking for you because the new Master Chariji will be here in two days." I went to see Chariji and told him that I would be going to India the following week. I asked him if I could come and see him in Madras (Chennai). He said, "Of course. Come on the eighth of August."

[When I arrived in India], I went to Auroville for a month because my mother is a disciple of The Mother (see Alfassa, Mirra 1878-1973 in references). I had friends there and ended up spending a month in Pondicherry, Auroville. I came here on the eighth for ten days at the foot of the Master. This was in 1985. I was made preceptor in 1988 in Cormet another time that Master came to France for three months.

Kim: So, thirty-five years as a preceptor abhyasi? You were never tempted to join Auroville and the Mother?

No. I went to Auroville with my mother's friends and had a very good time. It was marvelous, but I felt the atmosphere was not for me. They were building the Matrimandir at the time (see references and resources) and there was a lot of tension. The tension was so bad, I left Auroville to go to Pondicherry to study the yoga of the eyes. That is my job: to improve sight.

Kim: So you were waiting to meet Master?

I was waiting to meet Master.

Kim: Did you know immediately that it was right?

Yes, and then I never again left. When I returned to Sahaj Marg, my heart told me it is the simplest, purest and most efficient path.

Kim: It sounds like you were born with this spiritual hunger?

Yes.

Kim: For me, I didn't have that experience. My world fell apart.

That was my husband's experience.

He [Master] is also very good at cleansing. If you're suffering, he's very efficient at purification for removing the pain.

During my childhood, I was unhappy inside. I wanted to be a nun, so this must have been from karmic lives. Every time my heart opens, every time the love comes out, there is love for him, love for God; and that love is received.

Here is an anecdote, an example. In Atlanta, I entered a room where there were a lot of computers. Master was there in front of a computer. I was standing behind him and I was just thinking how much I loved him and how grateful I was to him. No word was said. Then he took one of those chocolate Mars candy bars and handed it to me. There were no looks or anything.

Kim: So do you think everybody can have that kind of personal connection?

I think everybody has it. I know many people who have that.

Kim: I don't have any kind of personal relationship. He doesn't know who I am.

This is what you think. He sees all hearts. It took me a long time to believe it but now I am convinced it is so. He's connected to all hearts.

Kim: Should I be nervous that he will know my secrets?

No, there are no secrets. The more your heart is open and the more you are sincere and authentic, the happier he is and the more he can help you. Don't hide anything. You can't hide anything. Even if you wanted to, you cannot. It's impossible.

Kim: I sometimes wonder how they put up with us bumbling human beings.

He's a Master. He has a universal superior consciousness. He answers everyone.

Kim: Did you ever feel any kind of conflict between religion and spirituality?

Several times and for some months. I was born Christian and was very connected with Christ and the Virgin Mary, but now they're all here. It's the same energy of love; <u>there is no difference.</u>

Kim: Do you think they're working together to help us?

Working together? Sure.

Kim: Do you think that people who are Christian feel that it's a kind of blasphemy against Jesus Christ?

No, because they're working together; they're all love. Where there is love, there's no blasphemy. Babuji often talks about it in *The Whispers* (see *Whispers from the Brighter World*, 2010, 2012, 2013 by Chandra, Shri Ram in References). I always felt that, but in *The Whispers* it has been well described. Jesus Christ is a big Master.

Kim: So what do you think about Sahaj Marg and the future of the world? Do you think it will have an impact?

Yes, I'm sure it will have an effect. I have had a lot of hope for the future since *The Whispers* came out. For those who remain, their consciousness will rise and it will be higher than it is now. Sahaj Marg will then truly take its place, especially if they open according to the way it is described in *The Whispers*. It is inevitable that *The Whispers* will be spread.

Kim: You know, I talk to my family and I'm convinced that we are close to a time of great catastrophe. There are a lot of programs on TV about Doomsday with many saying they don't really see how the world is going to go in a good direction.

You have to do your own work, purify yourself and advance the elevation of the soul and take who you can with you. Use The Whispers to advance and just keep moving forward to elevate the consciousness. Those that can, will follow. And those that can't, cannot be forced.

Kim: Is that what 'surrender' is?

I don't know if that's what it is, but I live it that way.

Kim: What is 'surrender' to you? I'm interested about 'surrender' and 'constant remembrance.'

'Surrender' is really to listen to what's going on inside and what's going on in life. Listen to your heart – it tells you what you should do, and [what it] wants you to do. Do not go down your own path or do what you think you wish to do. Rather, [do] what your heart tells you and what your Master tells you.

To 'surrender' is to understand that the Master loves us and he wants what's best for us. Everything that happens to us is perfect for us.

What works for me in constant remembrance is the permanent constant of the divine inner presence in our heart. The subtle divine is my Master within.

Kim: What about your brain? Does it ever get in the way?

The mind does what it has to do; it thinks. But I can still feel in my heart. It's not a thought, it's a feeling inside. Now I'm speaking to you, and I can still feel in my heart. So I think this is constant remembrance. For me, this is not in the mind; it's in the heart.

Kim: Do you think people have to learn how to control their mind?

Not the mind, but you can control your thoughts. When they are bad thoughts, you try to cancel them out. It's an attitude, a way of being. Constant remembrance is more remembering inside your heart. It's nothing to do with controlling your thoughts.

Kim: Do you have any advice for someone just starting to seek something more?

Are you asking what Sahaj Marg can bring to them?

Kim: It wouldn't have to be Sahaj Marg. Unlike you, I haven't tried anything else. I feel like I asked for help and this came and I'm not going to question it. I live with two 20-year olds; they're interested in other things. Is spirituality something that comes to people when they hit a certain age? Is it something that we seek when we have tragedies?

All humans should be interested in spirituality, but it is not the case yet. Just pray. When it is their time, it will happen. The fact that you're inside [meditating] is already working on them, that's for sure. Under the surface, the work is being done.

Kim: Do you have any advice for somebody who is just starting? I bring this up because right before I came here I spoke with my girlfriend. What she thought would make her happy in life didn't work out. She has everything she ever wanted, yet she is not happy. We went out, we talked and I recommended meditation, sittings and maybe that there's a bigger purpose in life. I haven't heard from her since. If she had been there with you, what would you have said to her?

No more than you, you did well. It's working; Master hasn't left her. Think about her from time to time; you cannot do more than that. Sahaj Marg is universal, but not every human being is ready. It's very pure; it's very simple. You have to be <u>really</u> ready. Maybe it's [your suggestion] was too strong, too strong.

Kim: Readiness to learn.

Readiness to grow.

Chapter 4

Lifelong Search

Senior

Indian, male, early 90's, retired army officer

Preface: I first noticed Senior on his way to get a fresh coconut near the ashram gate. He was moving along in his electric wheelchair much faster than I could possibly walk. This ritual seemed to be part of his morning routine, just after meditation has ended. I had noticed him before on the ashram grounds and wondered if he lived there full-time. One day, I met him just outside the apartment flat I was sharing while at the ashram and we struck up conversation. I was interested to hear he is Indian but has lived many years in Australia. I was even more intrigued to learn that he has spent many years actively searching for a guru. He graciously agrees to an interview and we make an appointment.

We meet one hot afternoon in his small flat, which he seems to share with another older gentleman. A large photo of Chariji dominates the area above his desk. Besides the desk, bed, and a chair on which I am perched, there is little else but books in his half of the room. There seem to be many, many books, and most look as if they are in the process of being read. Now in his early 90's, Senior begins the interview by talking about his lifelong search for a guru. This is an intriguing and new notion for me; I simply haven't imagined organizing my life around a search for a spiritual guru, but he clearly has. He discusses his move from Australia to live full-time at the ashram as well as his life plans. He gives frank and stirring responses when asked about death and spirituality. He encourages us to remember the body is just "dust to dust" and our real goal, while alive, is the soul's evolution and eventual mergence with the divine. Senior will give you much to consider.

Kim: Could you begin by telling us a little about yourself?

I am 91 years old and Indian-born. My parents were spiritual people. In the Indian system, religion is not something which you practice like church on Sunday. Religion is the way of life in India. So I grew up in a family where my mother and father were people who were born in the Hindu faith. They believed in God, of course, but they also believed in a way of life – how to live an honest and moral life and how to bring up a family.

My mother's father was a landlord who educated my mother in the traditional lore of India. By 'lore,' I mean stories of Mahabharata, the war, Ramayana, the scriptures and other traditional lore.

I was born with a silver spoon in my mouth, my grandfather being a Squire of the place. I have never known what 'want' is. So it's my weakness that I've never experienced poverty. That's a great weakness for me. I wish I had experienced it.

In my family tradition, we always had a family guru. That was traditional; my grandfather's guru became my father's guru and so on, by tradition. So, my father had a guru, my mother had a guru, and I grew up with the belief, from childhood, that 'you must have a guru.' When I grew older, when I began to understand things a bit, I began to feel inside me that a guru is something which is essential for human life even though I did not know what purpose the guru serves. The answer came from certain verses in Sanskrit which describe a guru. One of the verses, for instance, says that a guru is the only one that can give you salvation. I believed in that very strongly, right from when I was a boy, a teenager.

I am not young now, you know. I lived through the Second World War. When the war ended, I was already a young officer in the Indian Army. Civil administration in India was in chaos; it took me to service in Burma.

Kim: How did you become interested in Sahaj Marg, in particular?

Because I believed in a guru, I joined a spiritual organization in Calcutta, where I lived. That was the Ramakrishna Mission, which is also in the United States and is worldwide. There is a man named Vivekananda, who was a guru of that Order. In that Order, they believe that God became Incarnate in the form of Ramakrishna and His chief disciple was Vivekananda who is also a patron saint of our Sahaj Marg (see references and resources at the end of this book). I was a great admirer of Vivekananda. I was a great reader and read a lot of his books. I used to admire him, follow his teachings, and so on. That's how I eventually came to Sahaj Marg. I joined the Ramakrishna Mission and I had a guru whom I liked in that Mission. He initiated me and then made me a member of that system. It included meditation also – that's how I learned meditation – [but] then he passed away. His successor did not appeal to me personally. I had no rapport with that man, so I abandoned it. I did not owe loyalty to anybody. Even though I was not actively pursuing, I still had the feeling that I needed a guru and I felt that a person without a guru is like an orphan. I felt orphaned. Without a guru, your life is useless.

At age 29, I got married to a Christian lady, settled in Delhi and reared three children, three daughters. When we separated, I was living in Australia. Since I was free – I had no ties, my daughters were grown up and married and so I had no family responsibility – I went back to India from Australia.

I lived in an ashram run by a learned lady. She knew the Indian scriptures – the Upanishads, the Vedas. She knew them. She had a very beautiful singing voice. She was running this beautiful temple on the mountain. I spent about six weeks or so there and then I asked, "Will you be my guru?" She said no. She said, "I am not your guru. Your guru is in the south of India. You will find your guru when the time comes [but] not here in the mountains."

Kim: About how old were you then? Maybe 30s, 40s?

I was about 50.

So I came back disappointed and I became dejected. There's an Indian tradition that 'when the disciple is ready, the guru knocks at your door.' So I believed, but I had never heard any door knock[ing] anywhere and I thought that this life was a wasted life. It was better to start another life. This life is wasted, but I can't take my life so I have to live it out. Then I drowned myself in books and studies and so on.

I tried Buddhism, went to a Buddhist monastery and did Buddhist meditation. I went to Sri Lanka; saw the Buddha's tooth in the Sri Lankan monastery, [but] nothing transpired after that in Buddhism.

At this stage, when I was in Australia, living in books, but dejected because I had no guru, a man turned up in my life. He was a white South African gentleman who used to sell books in Perth, Western Australia, where I lived. I came to know him because of books. One day, he came to me and he produced this book, My Master (Rajagopalachari, 1989), with a photo of Babuji on the top page. He said, "Look here. Have you seen this man? He is a famous saint of India." I said, "Famous saint? No, I don't think I know him. But India is crawling with saints. There's no shortage of saints in India." So I left him. I ridiculed him. Then he says, "No, this man is serious. I've read it, but there are certain parts of it I don't understand. I would like you to read it and I would like to discuss it with you." So I said,

"Okay. Leave it there." I had a pile of books on my table. I put it to the bottom of the pile and I went to bed.

I used to read a lot at bedtime. I was reading my novels and suddenly the thought came to me that this man brought a new book. I wondered what it was like, so I pulled it out from the bottom of the pile and read a few pages. First of all, the photo of Babuji – not the photo on the front cover, but the first full page inside the book of Babuji where he is offering something with the palms of his hands – that's a beautiful picture. That photo attracted me. I felt strongly pulled, like a magnet. It held my gaze for a while. Then I started reading. I read only a few pages and my heart started telling me, "This man is speaking the truth. This man is speaking the truth. He has the truth. He has the truth." I read till about 2 o'clock in the morning, then went to bed. The next morning, I finished the book. I said, "I must see this man. This is the man. This is the guru that I need. He has the truth. I have to find this man." He was in India and I was in Australia.

I saw that the publisher on the back of the book was P. Rajagopalachari, Parthasarathi Rajagopalachari, Alwarpet. I made note of that address, the address of the publisher. So I wrote a letter to this publisher guy, but I also knew that most publishers don't reply to letters. I didn't have much hope but I said, "This is the only thing I can do." Lo and behold! Within three weeks, I got a reply to that letter, and that bowled me over. I wrote to him and introduced myself. I said, "I am a spiritual seeker" and I gave my story, my history, and I said, "I am in need of a guru and I think the guru that you have written about is my guru. He's the guru that I need. So please give me his contact number in India." In fact, I was so convinced about this business that I had booked the ticket from Australia to India to see this Parthasarathi, the writer. When he replied to me, I saw his address, so I booked a ticket. I said, "I'm going to go to this man and ask him to direct me to his guru." He wrote back to me, but didn't say a word about his guru. Not a word. The letter had said that P. Rajagopalachari is in Ram Chandra Mission. So I concluded that maybe his guru is alive [and] he's the president.

Anyway, (see my vanity!), I said to myself, "This man is the disciple. He is talking about his master." So I was thinking. Then Chariji said in the letter, "We have a Mission in Australia and also in New Zealand." He gave me the names and addresses of the disciples. "These are our disciples. Please contact them. They will guide you further." I didn't like it. What to do? That was all that was available. So I didn't reply. I left it. I said, "If a guru has to happen, let the guru come." Within a week, I got a letter from Sister Xxx. She wrote to me saying, "I am in charge of Australia." Blah, blah, blah. "I understand you're an abhyasi." She got the story wrong. "I understand you're an abhyasi, so please register your details with me. Contact so-and-so." So I ignored that letter. I thought these are all certainly third or fourth generation down. They're no use. So I did not reply. This is my vanity.

Then she said, "In Perth, where you live, there are a husband and wife who are abhyasis. They are from Singapore. They live there. This is their contact." So I called that number. He wasn't there. He had shifted, but I was given the telephone number to where they had moved. I rang him and he sounded very encouraging and enthusiastic. He used to work in a hospital in Perth. Yes, he was an abhyasi, his wife was a teacher, and he was very glad to meet me. He said, "I will come to your house in the afternoon when my shift is over." Sure enough, at 3 o'clock, he turned up at my door.

He turned up at my door and he said, "So you're interested in my Master?" I said, "Yes." He said, "I've got many books for you to know about Babuji." Then he gave me more knowledge about the system. The next day, he brought me some books about the Mission and Babuji. I was very happy because I had the books and I started devouring them in my own time. I read them and was convinced that this system, the Sahaj Marg system, seemed to be the right one for me. There is real truth in this. Babuji must have passed it on to his successor, Chariji, and he has written about it, so maybe Chariji has the truth. So I wanted to meet Chariji. I booked myself a ticket for the beginning of December, 1995.

His private secretary still lives here [at the ashram in Manapakkam, Chennai] now. She took shorthand notes of Master's work. So I sent an email to Chariji to bypass her. Chariji replied – not directly, but via the secretary. She said, "Master says that you need not come to India to be introduced to the system. You can be introduced in Australia itself. Get in touch with Sister Xxx [in Australia] and she will do the needful." So I couldn't get rid of this Sister Xxx. I was disappointed again. I said, "No, I'm not going to listen to this woman. I'm going to plant myself there on his doorstep and see what he does. Let him say no to me. I will challenge him."

Strangely enough – this is how coincidence comes, synchronicity – because, within a few days, another letter came. Sister Xxx wrote saying, "I have never visited Perth. Although I'm in charge of Australia, I've never visited Perth. I have decided to visit Perth for the first time. I'm going to stay with the preceptor and his wife in their home, on so-and-so date, for the weekend. So please make it convenient to come meet me there. Bring your friends, if you wish." So, now I knew that this is the message that's coming through. I made it a point [to meet her].

I took my South African friend and another friend. The three of us went there and we got there a little late. We found the talk had already started. She was sitting on the arm of the sofa, very informal, and she was talking. But what she spoke – I knew that it was the same thing that Babuji says, in her own way of expression. I knew that it was the truth. My heart started telling me, "Say yes, say yes, say yes." Very clearly, I heard this three times. "Say yes, say yes, say yes." So when the talk was over,

10-20 minutes later, she said, "That's about it. That's what Sahaj Marg is. If you want to think about it, we have some literature. It's right over there. You can read it. We are going to have a coffee break, so please help yourselves to coffee and browse through those books. If you have any questions, you can ask." So I went to her. I said, "Yes, this is the way I want. I will join." She was delighted.

She started me off. She said she would come that same evening to do the first sitting, and the next day and the next day – three days I took my sittings, successive days as they do. My impression of that sitting was that I was knocked out. I didn't know what was happening. I was lost.

Kim: From the very first one?

My first one. I was lost.

Anyway, I told her, "I want more sittings like the sitting you gave." "Well, if you want more sittings, you have to come to Sydney. I'm in Sydney." I said, "I'll come." She said, "Welcome." I went to Sydney. Her little daughter gave up her bedroom for me. "You'll sleep there. Stay as long as you like. Meet other preceptors here. There are two other preceptors here. Feel free." I stayed there for two weeks or so, came back, and booked my ticket to go to India. I said, "I must go and see their Master. I must see the Master face-to-face. I'm going to do that."

I was given a letter of introduction, arriving in the morning mid-January, 1996. At that time, Master was living at the top end of the cottage. Half the house was Master's and the other half was the meditation hall. I can show you the location. So I went there and outside, as usual, at Master's cottage, there were a lot of people milling around. I took my letter of introduction and gave it to the doorman. "Please, I have come from Australia." In ten minutes, the doorman came and asked for me.

I put my hand up. "Please come in." Everybody's looking at me, waiting, thinking, "Who's this guy?" Anyway, I went inside. They were waiting for me and I walked inside. It was so beautiful. Master had a big desk. He was sitting at a desk and it was at the entrance door. Master was sitting there and the desk was across there and his secretary was sitting on his right with a shorthand book. Master is sitting with a big pile of letters in front of him. When I walked up, he looked up at me. I went in front and did *pranam* (blessings, a greeting) to him. He looked me up and down. "Master, why are you looking at me up and down?" "So, you are Senior." "Yes, sir." "You live in Perth, Australia. Welcome, welcome. How long will you stay?" I said, "Master, I have a three months' ticket but I can extend it if necessary. I'm not limited by time." "Good, good." Then he ignored me. I sat down.

There are so many coincidences here. I sat down and there were a lot of foreign abhyasis, Indian abhyasis, men, women - all sitting there. It was ten minutes before nine o'clock in the morning. Master got up and looked at his watch. It was time for satsangh. Satsangh was next door in the meditation hall. I was sitting near the door. I got up. As he was passing me, he looked up. He stopped. He looked back at me and said, "I want to give you a sitting." Just like that. I said, "Okay, Master. When?" He said, "Come this afternoon at four o'clock. Here at this dorm." Now, my heart is going thump-thump-thump.

I went there. There was another guy from Bangladesh and myself. He was also asked to come. We went in at 4 o'clock into the same room and we sat on the floor. Master sat on a chair facing us and gave a sitting. I was lost. When I came out of the sitting, I felt like a zombie. A zombie. I didn't know where I was. I mean, I knew where I was physically, but really speaking, I didn't know where I was. [It was] like being in another world, so to speak. I went back to my room, had dinner and everything. It was like I was hypnotized. It took about three or four days for me to get out of this mummy state.

The next morning, I was sitting in the yard there, on the same green bench, and somebody came and sat next to me, a young chap I didn't know. He introduced himself to me. After a few minutes of conversation, he said to me, "Would you like to travel with Master in June?" It was a question out of the blue. I had heard Master's plan to travel in June to Europe and America. I heard his travel agent discussing the dates and everything. In my heart of hearts was the utmost desire to be able to travel with him. I knew that Master does take abhyasis with him when he travels and Sister Xxx had told me in Sydney, "If you get a chance, go with him." Would I be so lucky? This guy comes out of the blue and says to me, "Do you want to go to Europe? If you want to go, Master says yes. All you have to do is meet this travel agent guy and he will fix it." It was a miracle, of course, for me! I also got to travel with him in Australia and New Zealand. I have many special memories from the first time I travelled with Master while I was living in Australia. [I was] in his entourage, with 12-15 people; we used to go wherever he went.

I have another special memory to share. In April one day, I was told by an abhyasi, "Master wants to see you. Go and see him in his cottage." So I ran. Master said to me, "Sit down. Tell me your details. How old are you? How is your health? Can you travel?" I said, "Yes, I can travel by car." He said to me, "How would you like to become a preceptor?" I said, "Master, if you think I'm worthy of it. I'm old but I'm physically fit. I would be delighted to serve you." "All right." Then he fixed a date and all that, then gave me the first sitting within a few days. He said to me, "Now if you take more sittings, there's a Danish lady named Xxx. She was Babuji's first preceptor... Go and meet her and she will give you the further sittings. Two sittings a day, morning and evening."

So I went to her. She was delighted. She gave me a sitting. She told me after the sitting, "Go home and sleep." Going home means sitting on the floor [in the male dormitory] under the mosquito net, and that's what I was doing. This went on. She gave me seven sittings. Then she told me, "You are ready. I'll tell Master that you're ready." She told Master. I was told to go for a final sitting to Master in 'Gayatri,' where he used to live, his personal home, so I went there. I was told to bring a box of sweets. With the sweets, I went there. I had to be there at six o'clock. Ten [minutes] to six, the gate of Master's door opens. The Nepalese guard opens the door, lets me in, and says, "Sit here on the verandah." At five to six, the door opens from inside and Master opens the door, "Come in."

I went inside. Those days, he used to use a rocking chair. He sat in the rocking chair and I was sitting at his feet. I didn't utter anything at all. After a few minutes, when he said, "That's all." I woke up. He said, "Come with me." I stood up and followed him. At the far end of the room, there was a big blue statue of Lord Krishna. We went to it; he took the box of sweets, opened it, held it up in his hand and offered it to Lord Krishna most reverentially. The devotion that I saw in his eyes as he opened them is something extraordinary. I felt a huge lump in my throat and tears in my eyes just to see that offering that he was making. He was making *Prasad* (divinized food; see glossary) and I was crying. I was crying just to see that devotion. I stood like that in meditation and then he came away, broke a piece, put it in his mouth, put another piece in my mouth, and said, "Take these bits. Go to satsangh in the morning and stand at the door. When satsangh is over, distribute this for the abhyasis there as they leave."

Kim: Do you feel that you've changed since you started Sahaj Marg? How have you changed?

Yes. There was a huge change. What we call 'materiality' in Sahaj Marg language no longer interests me. I am no longer interested in material things. For example, I don't want to go to a cinema or see a movie, I don't want to eat an ice cream, things like that. I know now that spirituality is the essence of my life and, to be spiritual, to put yourself in a spiritual condition, to remain in a spiritual condition, is the way of life to be. I have learnt it and I have acquired it. I have acquired that habit of retiring within myself to remain in a spiritual state. That's the change that I've had.

Kim: You don't need to answer this if you don't want to. Is your goal liberation? To not have to come back, to not have to have another life?

Liberation is not my goal. For me, whether I have another life or not, is not of any consequence. To me, my goal is to be One with the Master because I know the God (divinity, as we say) is in Master, in Chariji. So when I die, I want to be united with him. I know that I will probably be going to the Brighter World. That's if I'm privileged enough and I'm not reborn. So I will be waiting there for him – of that, I'm sure. There's no question. My goal is simply to be united with him, to be merged in him. So, my real goal is to merge.

Kim: Are you afraid of death?

No.

Kim: Have you never left Manapakkam (Chennai, India) since you came here and became a prefect? Have you never gone away?

When I was a prefect, I was living in Australia. I moved from Australia to here about two and a half years ago. I realized, in Australia, I was living a material life and life didn't have much meaning. I said, "Why am I wasting my time here? I'm not serving any useful purpose. I want to serve Master." So I came to India and I told Master, "Master, I want to move from Australia to be here under your feet." He said with surprise, "Are you sure? You have your family there, your friends there;

your whole social life is there. How are you going to give all that up? Think it over. Don't give me an answer emotionally. Think it over."

I went back the next day having thought it over and slept over it. When I went back to find him, he was preparing to give a sitting. After the sitting, when he was going back to his room, I stood up and said, "Master, may I have a word?" He said, "Yes?" I replied, "I want to come here and stay with you at your feet in the ashram." Once again, he looked me up and down and then he paused for a minute or so, and then he said, "Okay." I asked, "When can I come?" He replied, "Whenever you like. Physically arrange things and send me an email and I will get the manager here to organize a place for you."

Kim: Wow! What did your family think?

[Members of the] family had different views. The eldest daughter – she is an abhyasi, but doesn't practice. She told me, "If you leave us and go, you will be disloyal to us because you have your family here and you're abandoning your family – your children, your grandchildren. Don't you think you have a responsibility towards us, to be part of our life?" I replied, "No. However, I will miss the grandchildren." She was unhappy, really unhappy, and she just turned her face away and left disappointed.

My second girl didn't mind. She said, "I hope you'll be visiting us again. We may not be able to come to India to see you. I hope you'll be visiting us again." The youngest one said, "Dad, go if that is what you really want." I'm in touch with her on Skype. She said, "I will come and visit you." She has been to visit me since on several occasions.

Kim: Do you have any advice for someone who's just starting to think about spirituality, somebody who may not have your benefit of a family upbringing in spirituality, maybe? What would you say to a young person, or to anybody, who's starting to question the purpose of life?

I would say to such a person, "Have you ever thought of what is going to happen to you when you die? The Bible says, 'Dust unto dust.'" "Do you think about what's going to happen? That you're going to go six feet under and then that your bones will perish slowly in the earth and that's that? Don't you think there's something more to life than just 'dust to dust'? Just think about that and follow your heart. Whatever your heart says, do. If your heart says whatever you're doing is the right thing, then do it. When the time is ripe, your time will come.

You and I cannot anticipate, cannot hope, and you can't do anything beyond just putting a seed inside and that seed is the thought of the afterlife. Afterlife is the most important thing, as all men know. But they must realize it – the afterlife. When their afterlife thought comes, then everything will fall into place.

Kim: You know Master is getting older. His health isn't very good. Do we need to worry about the future?

If Master is going to go to the Brighter World, giving up His body, the fate of the Mission is well in the hands of his successor, Brother Kamlesh Patel. So whatever happens physically to Master, the Mission will go on through the hierarchy. I have no worries about his human body.

In fact, in one way I would be happy if he leaves his body. Ask me why.

Kim: Why?

It is because the Master has been long wanting to leave this world. He does not want to stay. He finds this bondage to the body too tiresome and he wants to go to the feet of his Master as soon as possible.

We as abhyasis, however, pray that he not leave us, that he stays with us. We're simply being selfish. We don't want him to go. We love him. What will we do without him? It's nonsense. If you love him, you must love what is good for him. What do you think is good for him? Is it good to leave his material body, with all the ailments and all the time suffering? He suffers greatly, you know. I cannot consciously say I don't want him to go. I pray to Babuji to take him as soon as possible.

Kim: Is it your belief that, in the Brighter World, all of the venerables are working together to help us humans? You mentioned Babuji, some people say even Jesus Christ, Mohammed…

They're all united. They're all united for the liberation of humans.

Kim: Do you see Sahaj Marg as kind of a hope for the future? Here we are, polluting the world, starting wars, focusing on materialism or violence. For young people in particular, I think you know it's a really hard time to be alive and feel hope. Some people say Sahaj Marg is really the hope for the future and even have talked about Babuji saying the genetic make-up of human beings would go through a mutation, helping us to evolve. Do you have any comments on that?

I know that the material body does change its DNA and that is a physical phenomenon. [There is] nothing special about that. It's just like our skin is changing over time slowly, like that. So it's not a big deal at all.

More importantly, spiritually, it may not be Sahaj Marg. It may be other systems. I can't say that Sahaj Marg is the only system in the world. It is not true. There are other systems even I am not aware of. For example, Babuji has said, in other planets, every planet has its own environment; living beings there, maybe they're more evolved than us. They have their own lives. The universe is very large and very vast. We can't possibly fathom what it contains. So, there are many things going on other than Sahaj Marg. I accept all that. It's accepted intellectually and mentally, but my limited understanding is that Sahaj Marg surely can do it.

Kim: Do you have anything else to add? Anything else you would want people to know or to think about?

The only thing I want people to think about is their afterlife. 'Is there an afterlife? If there is, what is the afterlife?' Just think about it. *Samskara* (see glossary) really is a program, like a computer program. It is almost like a mechanical thing because samskara is something that has to run according to schedule, like something that is set; it is not within your control. Each person has his own samskaras – programs he has set for himself before taking birth. In other words, I believe that, when I die, if this is not going to be my last life (I hope that is not true), I would have a period of time, an inter-dimensional gap, where I would pause and I would reflect on how I want to be born in the next life. For example, such things that I have missed in this life, people that I have not forgiven in this life, prejudices that I have had which I want to get rid of… kind of an agenda. So, you reflect on an agenda for your next life. That is the period of preparation for the next life. In other words, we pre-program our next life before we are reborn.

Buddhism is a system. They say that, when a man dies, it takes 40 days for him to be reborn. That 40-day period is time ad infinitum. Here you will re-program and decide what you want to do in that period because, after that 40 days, you have to be reborn again. It is similar to what we have.

Kim: Yes. I think the Tibetans have the <u>Book of the Dead</u>, too.

In the Tibetan <u>Book of the Dead</u> (see references and resources Evans-Wentz, 1927), they have this idea too. The Buddhists have two schools, the Northern School and Southern School.

The Northern School is the Northern, and the Southern School is the one in Sri Lanka, Cambodia, Vietnam and Thailand. They again have a different system.

In real life, we get deflected because there are so many distractions in real life as it unfolds – attractions and prejudices, over and over again. This is the tragedy of human life. Why do we have repetitions of birth and death, birth and death? If we are fortunate to have a guru, we stick to the guru and we allow the guru to keep us on course. He keeps us united with God. Uniting with God is the real purpose of human life. In fact, the first line of our prayer says, 'Thou art the real goal of human life' because we have come away from our home. That [uniting with God] is the whole purpose of my life.

Kim: So what if you're 84 years old and you don't have a guru?

The longing is still there, but you don't know what to do. You don't have a guru, but your longing is there. Your longing can't stop. In fact, you will remain Kim all your life – birth after birth, birth after next birth, ad infinitum. Going nowhere.

Kim: Do you think you have to be pure to be spiritual?

Purity is a consequence. It happens. Impure is… uncomfortable. Purity is a consequence; like happiness. Happiness is a consequence of a safer mind. You can't disguise happiness. You can't give a definition of happiness. It is there – joy, sorrow. Just like that, I think. It's a state.

Kim: To be content – is that one of your goals at this stage in your life? Just to be content?

To be content is my natural condition. I am naturally content. So it's not a goal. Again, to be content is a consequence of my practice. I say it with all humility. I mean, I am content because why should I be discontent? There's nothing to make me discontent. I have my Master. I am following him. I know in my heart of hearts that, if I stray, I come to know that I'm straying. He needs to make sure – it is his job – making sure that I'm on the right path. I cooperate with that. Thank you.

Chapter 5

"Contaminate" Your World with Love and Beauty

Virginia

French born in N. Africa living in India, female, 40's, dancer and designer

Preface: Virginia's story was supposed to be in this book, I believe, as was her son's story (Jean Baptiste), which is in the first book of the series. They just happened to be in the garden where I conducted one of the very first interviews. They were in the garden first, resting on a Sunday afternoon while waiting for the next satsangh (group meditation). They had driven very early from Pondicherry, a distance of several hours by car, and were spending the day at the ashram before heading home after evening satsangh. They kindly shared the sofa space and eventually became drawn into our interview conversation. Immediately after, I asked Virginia if I could interview her, already intrigued by her depth of thought and richness of experiences. She agreed, as did her son Jean Baptiste, so three interviews happened quite naturally when I was anticipating only one!

Virginia is lovely, with reddish blonde hair that falls in waves to her shoulders. Dressed in feminine cottons and lovely fabrics, she shows her gorgeous fashion sense, combining practicality with beauty and West with East. She is a fashion designer, I learn later, making and selling one-of-a-kind fashions. Virginia tells the story of being drawn to India as a young woman and, at age 22, meeting Master while making money to save up to study dance in Chennai. She was literally drawn to him on the job and would hide her apron and sneak away in order to meditate with him. When asked to relay any memorable experiences with Master, Virginia shares her experience of despair when thinking she would be separated from her children. She touchingly describes how Master intervened in her life in a very real sense. She advises us to follow our hearts and to work to become masters of ourselves.

Kim: Can you tell a little bit about your background? I know you speak French, but where are you from?

It's a difficult question because I was born in Africa, in North Africa in Casablanca, and grew up there until the age of 15. Then the French government asked all French people to come back to France because that was the agreement between Morocco and France in the 1980s. Therefore, my mother, father and sisters had to come back to France.

Kim: So you lost your first country in a way.

Yes, if you want to say so, but I always feel that there is a link between my origin and where I am now.

Kim: Now would be the time to recall any background, context, family influence, or any life experiences that have brought you to where you are now.

My father never wanted us to be part of any religion. He always used to say, "I don't believe in religion. We have no religion. When you are 18, if you want to choose, you are free to do so but, for now, we are not linked with any religion."

What happened is that I am in India because of my passion for dance. At the age of 21 or 22, I opened a magazine and I saw an article about a College of Fine Arts, [located in] Chennai in India. I had never heard about India before. I'd never read any books about India or Indian culture.

But what is very, very strange is that, when I look at photos from when I was 13, 14, or 15 years old, I used to draw a dot [on the forehead, where a third eye would go in Indian tradition] and my mother used to say "no, no, do a little dot near your eyes." She was talking about the beauty mark people would put near their eyes. So later on, I found it very interesting to see that I was doing this [marking a third eye] even though we had no contact with India and they had never told me anything about this civilization.

So my family was in France and I opened a magazine. I was passionate about dance but my father didn't want me to be a dancer; he wanted me to be like him in the theater. But I resisted and when I opened this magazine and I found the College of Fine Arts, Madras [Chennai], and I saw all these beautiful pictures of young women in different poses, I said "Wow! This is the dance. This is the dance that I was always longing for!" I had a big, big, big flash of realization. When I came home, my mother was the first one there and I told her "Mom I want to show you! I want to show you something. Look at this! Look, this is the dance! And this is the place where I am going to go now – India!" And she looked at me with big eyes and her mouth open and she said "India? It's not possible! You're not going to go to India." And I said, "Yes, Mom, look look! This is what I want to do! This is really what I have been craving since my childhood."

It was difficult. I needed money and I needed to earn that money very quickly because the audition was in June and it was already around April the year before. I needed to find money for three years for my diploma and plane ticket, everything. My mother was a very generous and very beautiful, kindhearted mother, and she looked at me and said "Virginia, if it is what you really want to do from the depths of your heart, I will help you. You don't have to worry about your plane ticket; I'll take care of that." She was not very wealthy so I knew that she was sensitive enough to see that this was something that was really important for me.

About two weeks later, the phone rang. I was there in the house when my mother picked up the phone and said "Yes, it's you. Yes, my daughter is looking for work. Yes, when? Oh great, yes! I'll call her." I came and she told me that it was a friend of hers and he has a big center called Cormet, located at the peak of a mountain in the south of France. He was looking for young people to come and work for three months. So I said, yes, I was interested. I spoke with him and we agreed I would go there. I only knew I would be cleaning, cooking, and doing whatever they asked me to do. After three or four months, I would receive a good salary that could help me on my travels. And so I went to work.

When I arrived there - I will never forget - in the evening, I saw all these people at a violin concert. But instead of looking at the violinist, they were looking in another direction. I was trying to figure out why there was a concert and somebody playing and why people were looking in another direction. I realized there was something there but I passed through the area very quickly because I had finished my work and was tired so went to sleep.

So all of this is to tell you that the starting point of me coming to India was my passion for dance, which led me to go to the first big seminar of Sahaj Marg in France of our Master Chariji and I ended up at a three-month seminar. I was 22 and I can say that this was my rebirth. I have a very, very, very strong feeling that I was born again during that summer.

Kim: Were you at an ashram?

It wasn't at an ashram. It was the first three-month seminar in Europe after the death of his own Master. Babuji Maharaj died in 1986, so this would be two years later, in 1988. It was given at the peak of an old Celtic, Druid place – very, very beautiful, at about 800 meters above sea level on the peak of a mountain.

Kim: Was Master Chariji there for the seminar?

Yes! The next day I was serving food and, through the glass window, I saw a man seated on the first floor but I could only see his back. I was serving food with the team when I saw this person there. I don't know why, but I left my station and asked someone to take care of the food as I had to go. I sat below his window and I looked at this person, seeing only his back. Then he turned and he looked down at me with these eyes big with surprise and I was surprised that he was looking at me! Then he made a sign with his hand calling me and I said, "Are you calling me?" and he said 'Yes, come' using his hands. I didn't speak a word of English. He was coming down the stairs and I was going up the stairs, and I didn't know who he was. But when I saw him, I remember that the first time I saw him was like meeting a great friend again or someone I was already very deeply acquainted with. He gave me a present and he said a sentence, which I only understood ten years later. This is the way I came to Sahaj Marg.

We were not allowed to meditate because I was working, so I had to hide to meditate. I would run to the fields, leave my apron somewhere, and I would join the meditation when I would hear the bell.

Kim: And you never looked back?

In what sense?

Kim: You left home...

I remember my father's words when I told him I was going to India. He said, "No, no I disagree totally. I disagree totally with your decision. You will be totally lost there and you will never come back." And he was right actually, because I never came back in the real sense.

When I came to India, I had a feeling that I was coming home. I arrived in Mumbai and I remember that I had a feeling of coming back home. But this is my personal story. I can only explain this because there is a thread, like when you weave a piece of cloth. I speak of cloth because I also design and it makes sense for me to speak of something that resounds in me. When you weave, you need different threads that you inter-weave like a tapestry. There was a very, very important thread and I intuitively followed that thread. I understood. It was something that was totally instinctive. I never looked for a Master; I never even knew that there was a Master! But I can remember that, in my childhood, as we didn't have any religion, I couldn't sleep if I hadn't done a kind of prayer. But I never knew about prayer so I used to do something like "protect my family, protect France, protect…" and I would go on like this, in bigger and bigger circles. Later on, I understood that it is linked [similar] to one of our practices in Sahaj Marg.

In my childhood, I had these visions and my mother was very scared of them. So, I always promised her: "Mom, I will find a magician." She would always come back to that point with me: "Did you find your magician?" And I would say: "Mom, I promised you I would find that magician." It's like a story for children but I like stories for children because they are innocent and pure. For me, I had a vision that, if I knew a wise person who could tell me about our stay on earth, and why there is life and why there is death, I could help my dear mother to go through her journey on earth.

Kim: So did your mother meet Master?

My dear mother… she just left the earth five months ago and she started meditation six months ago. She met our Master ten years ago, as well. It took her a while to understand but, at the end, she knew that she did not have to be scared of anything, that love was there. It's like a fairy tale but life is like a fairy tale. It just depends which side we look at.

Kim: And now you have two children?

Three children.

Kim: What is your situation now? Do you live in Pondicherry?

Yes. I live in Pondicherry near Auroville, where I am a volunteer teacher in school, in kindergarten and as a facilitator in art, dance and theatre to find awareness for the body through music and through Montessori. Montessori is very much linked with spirituality. Maria Montessori saw the infinite dimension of a child and she saw that, at an early age, a child is still totally connected with the Source. You may say, "What is the Source? What are we talking about?"

Most people love to have a newborn baby in their arms. Children are connected to themselves. They are totally in the present and they don't live in the future or in the past. This is their secret. Therefore, when they are connected to themselves, they have an immense knowledge, access to the total knowledge that has existed since the beginning of time.

I do not exaggerate. We see children who can do things that seem totally inaccessible for adults. A child is able to see, to do, to say, to feel, and to experience unlimited tools within himself and through the world he lives in. We only create obstacles to their learning because we have a fixed program for them. Therefore, their own program cannot be open to them when we push them into a fixed program. So if we respect the child for what he is, we see that the child can go far beyond any teaching.

Kim: A child's play is his work?

Yes. When he plays, he works and is totally absorbed. So when we work we should be like children. When we are really working in this way we can accomplish and be totally absorbed. That's what I'm doing now.

Kim: Is your volunteering a full time job and if so, is it because you are an Auroville resident?

No, I'm not an Auroville resident and I don't know if I will be because it's a little bit complicated, but that is another story. Auroville is a beautiful place on earth with a good number of people working together for change, but it is a reflection of our world as well. So it will take its own process. Right now, I am a volunteer and offer my work, which I am not paid for. I feel very fulfilled because I don't earn money. I am not doing this for money.

I feel we can link it to your question about Sahaj Marg and the connection with the environment and the social, which is: How can we, as tiny drops in the ocean, be together and create waves and create the ocean, actually? It's not a grand work but it is this small work that can create change in our DNA, our aspirations, and create a change in understanding [about] where we are going, where we came from and what we are.

Kim: How do you make ends meet?

That's a good question. It is not easy for me and I still have to understand how to link the two worlds together, materialism and spirituality. Our Master teaches us to live simply and not to have too many wants and [to] be more linked to our needs. I'm also learning to reduce my standard of living without losing my sense of contentment, but it's not so easy.

Kim: How long have you been in Pondicherry?

Almost ten years.

Kim: What brought you to Pondicherry?

I was working in an International School in the mountains around Kerala at 2000 meters. We decided it was too remote from the world. It was a good experience but I needed, as a dancer as well, to return to the artistic side to have more opportunities to meet artists. We decided on Pondicherry because neither of us likes big towns and it's not far from Chennai, where our Master lives.

By the way, he doesn't like to be called a "Master." He never wanted to be called a Master, and asked us not to call him "Master." He asked to be called by his name, which is Chari. We add a "ji," which means respect.

Kim: I called him "sir" and he didn't like that. He asked me to call him "brother."

That is interesting because it is about worship. People have a tendency to worship very easily. He never wanted that. He said, "I don't create disciples. I make people masters of themselves." It means you master only yourself. [The idea is] to master your own passion, to master your anger, to master your desires, to become the master of your life. This is what he teaches us.

Kim: Do you have any advice for someone new to the concept of spirituality?

For what the world is now I would say, "Follow your heart." I would advise all youngsters to read Antoine de Saint-Exupéry's The Little Prince, because, at one point, there is this beautiful sentence, "One can only see with the heart and the core essence cannot be seen with the eyes." Therefore, [practice] meditation – because in meditation, we learn how to look inside, not outside. Outside, you can be misguided by your senses, by your passions, by the way you were educated, by publicity put out by the government, by schools. But if you look inside and you meditate, you will know the truth.

Kim: Are there any interesting stories you want to share; memorable or funny?

It's not funny. Painful, but beautiful.

At one point, our children's father and I separated. He decided he would take the children with him to France and I was feeling very desperate about it. I didn't know what to do because I had to convince him that I, as the mother, should not be far from them. So I made the difficult choice to leave India, where my heart was. Part of my heart is here in India and part is there [France]. At that time, he wasn't ready to listen and I wasn't ready to fully understand the situation. In desperation, I went to Chariji. When he received me, I cried and accepted his handkerchief. He wiped my tears and asked me, "What is it?" I said, "The father of my children has decided to live in France and I don't know what to do. I have nothing in France; I don't know how I will live as we are not together anymore. For him it's easier; for me it's not." At that point, Master looked at me and said, "Leave the children with him." I looked at him and did not answer. I had tears coming from my eyes and everybody was silent in the room.

I left the room and felt I was almost losing my sanity. I had some very negative ideas; I climbed up to the third floor and felt like dying. I'm telling you this because maybe it can help others in desperate situations – and also, to understand the depth of the Master, of somebody who has mastered the world of spirituality.

Master left his cottage and walked one kilometer and arrived to where I was. Looking up, he saw me; it was just a one-second exchange, a glance of an eye. I came down and all my [negative] ideas went out of my heart.

Still, I had this situation. I came down [from the third floor] and the situation got worse. The departure was imminent and the situation was about to fall apart. The children were very excited to go. They didn't realize what was happening, as they were quite young. Everything was ready but, the day before the departure, our children's father put his passport in a cupboard by mistake. All the furniture had already been put on a ship and it had departed. So he was left with no passport or ticket. He rushed to the Consulate and they said they would prepare a new passport. It was the morning of the 24th of December and the Consulate was to close at 12 o'clock noon. He went there at 10:30 and they told him to return in an hour when it would be ready. Meanwhile he also got a new plane ticket. So he returned to the Consulate an hour later. He learned that, as they were issuing the passport, there was a power failure and all the computers went down. No passports were to be issued.

He returned home. He is a very, very wise person. He looked at me and said, "I want to tell you something. I'm sorry. I'm not going to Europe; I'm not going to France. I'm staying here and the children are staying here." He's still in India and we didn't become separated.

Kim: Is spirituality about surrender?

Spirituality is about nature. I'm so happy [my son] is going to do [an eco-science program] because it is the best link to watch and observe nature. In nature, everything is taken care of. The butterflies do not worry about where they will get their nectar from and the birds sing before dawn. Everything we are asked to do is by observing nature and so you can surrender, full of power in a passive attitude. This doesn't mean that you should let someone mistreat you. Do not mistake this. Understand that, in non-action, you're actually much more in the action than when you fight facing the event. In surrender it is to be present totally, in the conscious and not conscious. It is to accept suffering, to embrace it – not in a masochistic sense, but if something happens to you, acknowledge that event, take it in, and absorb it with as much love as you can. At first, I did not and even now sometimes I don't understand this. It's not easy, but reflect on it and allow nature to do what it has to do. Let nature guide you. Let nature show you the signs. Open your eyes and ears. See with the inner eye. This is how I understand surrender.

So let's all try to feel more, instead of reacting and going against... His grandfather and my father were both navigators and we used to sail on a 12-meter boat. My sisters and I were all very young, the three of us, 4, 5 and 7 years old. He [grandfather] never had any sons, so he would treat us like boys sometimes. He always taught us that, during a storm, do not keep the sail on. Sometimes we had to put the anchor on to drag the sand at the bottom, and keep the compass on [site]. We would take down the sail and just wait.

So through sailing, you can learn how to proceed when in difficulty. Never face a current if the current takes you in the opposite direction. You never go against a current. You allow the current to take you a little way away from your goal, but the idea is to be able to return to that place there. So knowing how to sail helped me navigate the "not so easy" oceans in my life.

The meaning of Sahaj Marg is the "natural path." Therefore, it is not something that we can impose on anybody. It is a way of living that comes from our good will and from our hearts. In times of disaster and extreme circumstances, you have to be able to create change. With us, it is the same procedure. If we do not face obstacles, sometimes the change does not happen.

We are at a time in the world where we have no choice. I feel the only choice we have is to be spiritual or we destroy ourselves. This [materialistic focus] started many, many years ago. It is insidious and has gone very smoothly in education, in business, in government, and in religion as well. I don't want to be controversial but I do want to point out the reality.

In India, the caste system that was so strongly implemented and followed for many centuries started as something to actually help people regarding their own talents and their own strengths, and not for manipulative means. What I observe in India now is that the caste system has become stronger and stronger and religion has become very manipulative with an emphasis on money. Religion has become a big business in India – and everywhere in the world. In India, men and women shave their heads to give it [the hair] to the Gods. And now this hair is afterwards sold all around the world to people to beautify themselves.

Priests are asking for more and more donations for any kind of a *puja*, for prayer, and they ask for huge amounts of money. The poor suffer the most because they are not well educated. They cannot go and become educated because they have no time after work. If they don't work, they starve. So this becomes a vicious circle. When we face a situation like this in a civilization, we know we have come to a point of almost no return. This is present everywhere.

I used to think India was the sacred land, the land for spirituality and the land for great masters. This was the case, but it is no longer, because India is now following American and European models. It has now become the social pattern to be what others are. That is now considered better than what is traditional. So with the caste system, it goes on and continues in this manipulative way and it also continues in a new way, such as in business. The new religion on earth is business. So you have these two tendencies in social behavior here in India. This is creating a disaster.

With the grace of our Chariji, we see inter-community marriage and arranged marriages, which are the doors to freedom for the citizens of this world. It is one of the solutions given. So you see this understanding between people even though they do not live or work in the same place - be they outcasts or very rich people. There are these kinds of unions happening. Therefore, there is hope for social change, at least for India. I would say that everything is in our hands and nothing is fixed.

So there is no disaster to come. On the one hand, we have the consequences of our actions but, on the other hand, we have the power to change the consequences of our actions.

Kim: So that is the hope of Sahaj Marg, to give us that hope?

Very much so. If we interact with our capacity to change, it's like quantum physics. When one cell changes, all the other cells change around it. So if you start the work with yourself, you are sure to contaminate the world around you with love and beauty. There is a lot of hope, actually, but we have to work hard.

Thank you for giving us the opportunity to exchange ideas.

Chapter 6

Mold Life From Your Inner View

Teresa

Spanish, female, 30's, musician

Preface: Teresa was pointed out to me after meditation one day in the great hall. I approached her, needing a prefect to do a 1:1 sitting with me. She was introduced as "someone who has a very pure heart." We make a time and place to have the sitting and she also kindly agrees to an interview. It is a beautiful sitting, although I am distracted with worries about how to format the book. Amazingly, one of the first things she tells me after we open our eyes is to stop worrying about the book, that she has "already seen it and it is beautiful, all done."

We meet after the 6:30 a.m. meditation and before the 9 a.m. begins, sitting on a bench near the playground outside the main steps to the meditation hall. Birds caw noisily in the trees above our heads and people stroll by on the main road between the ashram gate and the canteen. We smile at the loud birds and have to raise our voices for the tape recorder. Now a young woman in her early thirties, slim and winsome, Teresa shares with us her feelings of being connected with the Divine even as a young girl. She emphasizes her intuition that we are on Earth to follow a pre-determined plan, which will help each of us to evolve. She encourages us to start our search for spirituality early and to mold our lives based on the inner view, by listening to our hearts. She also explains how a spiritual life and improved sense of balance have helped her to deal with bullying experiences. Teresa is lovely and unique; I think you will enjoy her story.

Kim: Could you begin by telling us a little about yourself? How did you become interested in spirituality?

Since [I was] a very young girl, I was interested in knowing who I was and why I was here. I remember, when I was only four years old, asking my father, "But <u>why</u> am I here? What are we doing? Who are we?" and he was telling me, "Oh, don't worry about that. We only know when we die. So you should not get worried about that." But still, I had this, something inside, that <u>needed</u> to know who I was, and why, and what to do, and what meaning has life, and all this. I also remember, when I was in the sixth year of school (I was quite small); I had this idea that everything was a play, that we were all actors for each other. I also felt that nothing that was going on was that important, you know? The important thing was how we were relating to, <u>doing</u>, everything that was set up for us; <u>that</u> was the important thing.

I told my father [these ideas] and he told me, in an all-suffering, patient tone, "You are crazy. This is not how it is." (big laugh) So I actually said, "Maybe, okay maybe, I should just not worry about it." Actually, just a few months back, I realized [I was right]. There was a talk by Master, and he was saying exactly the same thing; that it's all a play.

I come from a very small village of about 200 people in Catalonia, Spain (about 100 km north of Barcelona). I turned 30 in January of this year. My father and my mother were educated in Christianity but they completely disagreed with it. Religion was imposed on them and they completely didn't want it so they didn't educate us [children] in a religious way at all. Maybe that's good, because I don't feel I have any conflicts: there was nothing imposed on me, so I am free to believe whatever I feel. There's nothing like, "Oh you have to pray." My grandmother, though, sometimes when I stayed with her she would make us pray at night, or she took us to church. Whenever I went to church, I somehow started talking to the images, to Jesus, and that was very beautiful for me. It was very special for me to go into a church. I felt the atmosphere was very calm; I felt really nice there.

Kim: So you've always been interested in spirituality?

Yes, but actually I didn't know what it was because I was never told, "This is spirituality." I was told, "This is religion. It's bad. Don't go there."

Kim: But you still felt in your heart there was something you were looking for?

Exactly. In fact, I had a very big problem, one of the biggest difficulties in my life when I had to decide what career I wanted to do. In high school, I was not the best student but I was quite a good student; I got good marks and teachers were telling me, "Oh, you should become a doctor, a physician." But actually, I knew I needed something else, something that would fulfill this emptiness inside. I was doing music at that time – I was better in my normal subjects but music seemed to fill some of that emptiness. While I was playing my musical instrument (cello), I felt that there was something else. I have to say that music has never been easy for me. I don't have the right (length) fingers, I don't have enough strength to press the strings, I don't have good rhythmic feeling that some people have – so for me to choose that [music] is not easy. It might have been easier to become a physician (laughs). But I needed that, you know? Something inside…I was telling my mother that I really needed something that fulfills me inside. So I went for that, and I got into a music school in London, a very good music school.

It was quite tough. The level and expectations were high and I had to work very hard but there, somehow, I started looking for spirituality. I decided to try a yoga class. I tried guided meditation. I started exploring with friends (yoga, meditation, wushu). Also, in that music school, they were giving us some tips for starting this kind of [spirituality], so that was very nice.

Then, by chance, just by chance, there was a guy in my last year (after I was a little bit into these things), there was a guy who, when we met all the students I thought, "Oh, he looks so familiar." I even winked at him like I knew him – but we didn't meet, we didn't speak.

One day, we were in a big hall and they were dividing, making us play with each other, so we can find the people with whom we could play together best. There was a pianist who played with me, then played with him and then she asked both of us to play together and set up a group (piano, cello, violin); so we ended up playing together. I didn't talk about spirituality with him (John). After a month or so, I was doing this hatha yoga and there was a guru coming from India, so I went to see him [the guru]. It was very strange. He had a big beard, dark hair, and was dressed very strangely – I didn't like him, actually. He was on stage, doing music and songs and all, and then he told everyone to set up a queue to meet him personally. I didn't want to do that but, by chance, I ended up being the third or fourth person in the queue. I wanted to leave but they told me, "No, you cannot leave; meet him first." When I got to him, he put his finger on my third eye and (breathed out) made a noise – and I felt he was really looking inside at all my chakras and cleaning everything. He was seeing me, my insides. Then he said, "Okay, you're not having an easy life but very soon you will find something that really fulfills your life and it will bring you to where you want to go. Then you will have a fulfilled life and everything will be fine." After that, I was crying for an hour or so.

That same night, we were playing a concert and my violinist friend John was there. He was the first person I met when I came from the guru and went to the concert hall and I needed to explain my experience to someone so I told him my story. Then he said, "Oh, are you looking for spirituality? Because I'm doing Sahaj Marg and it's a beautiful way of meditation." Soon after, I met the preceptor, a very nice woman, and she introduced me to Sahaj Marg. Since the first sitting, I knew that was it. I felt (I mean this is very personal because everyone feels in their own way), but I felt, even in the first sitting, [as I would if] a mother would hug me and hold me and say, "Ok, now you are safe." I knew it was my way.

I've been in the practice for six years now. At the beginning, I couldn't come to India because I had no money and my family didn't like it. They said it was this Indian thing, very strange. They are not spiritual and they just felt it was very strange.

Kim: Are they okay with it now?

Yes. Definitely. It's very nice. They are seeing the positive changes in me. They encourage me now. They are starting to be interested themselves.

Kim: So how have you changed?

I was very shy and unsure of myself, blaming myself for everything, thinking that I was not able to do things. [Now] I'm becoming much more secure, stronger – maybe not outside, maybe not my voice – but my heart is more loving. Now I think I can do what I want to do, what my heart tells me, you know? Before I thought I was not good, [that] I couldn't do things, but now I know I can do them!

Kim: What do you want to do?

(long pause) I want to become a better person. Sometimes it's not easy because sometimes you need to be confronted with people who are not that goodhearted. Yeah, sometimes it's tough. But sometimes you need it, because if we're always in a good place, everything is nice, how are we going to get better?

Kim: Would you have advice for young people who are just getting interested in spirituality or someone immersed in materialism but wanting to change?

Yes, yes. I would tell them to go into the spiritual path as soon as possible. When you are in a spiritual path, you start knowing where you're going, which goals you want to complete, so then your life can be molded with that inner view. Otherwise, you can get trapped. I don't know how to explain it but, if you start young, your life can be molded more easily than if you start when you are much older. I <u>wish</u> I could have started earlier, and I started quite young! But if I would have known Sahaj Marg before choosing my degree, maybe I wouldn't have needed to go into music and I could have gone into something not so difficult for me.

Kim: How important is it to be pure?

Well, I think if you go to places where people drink alcohol and all that, the atmosphere is really not good so, if you go there, it makes you feel bad. It's not only if you drink or whatever; being in this place can affect you. It's not that I put a norm [rule] on myself and I don't go; sometimes I want to go and I just go, but I need to protect myself and create this kind of a bubble inside, to protect myself. Be careful of where you go and how you think and who you are with.

Kim: How important is it to give up meat?

I do think it affects your inner condition – because if you are eating meat you are eating all this pain the animals have and it somehow creates this heaviness inside – but for me it was very natural to not eat meat. It was nothing imposed either, just like not going to discos and all that. It's not that I think it; it's just that I feel, "Oh, I don't want to go." With me, I started little by little. It was not something like, "OK, I am vegetarian now" and put [drew] a line. Still now, if I feel I went to eat a little bit of ham (because we have this jamón in Spain), I don't say I won't, but many times [I just] don't.

Kim: Do you have any memories or anything that stands out, anything you might want to share about your path toward spirituality?

Yes, for me, before becoming an abhyasi, I was in London studying – and in one day, many coincidences happened; many, many coincidences happened. By the end of the day I thought, "Oh, this magic of the world, please don't leave me." I called it magic or the universe – and it was <u>so</u> beautiful – like this feeling here, these birds or this light, the sun coming, beautiful moments. That day was <u>full</u> of beautiful moments and beautiful feelings inside. When the night arrived, there was a full moon. In my room, I had a window seat and, even though I prayed rarely, that night the moon was right there, shining in. With my knees on the floor, I prayed, "Oh, this magic of the world, please don't leave me because I need you – to guide me, to tell me why I am here, the reasons to live. Don't leave me because I really need you to guide my life. Please don't leave me. Stay with me always." There was this craving, to really feel that my life was guided.

A few months later, I met John and it all started. Someone told me later, "You know, when you pray deeply from your heart, your prayer is always heard and it's always answered." So, for Sahaj Marg finding me, I truly felt that came from [my] deep prayer. One day a few months later, I talked with John after meditation and he told me, "You know, today when I was coming to satsangh, I felt that I was meant to come to London so that you can find Sahaj Marg." Isn't that amazing? If we send out a cry for help, it comes.

Kim: Do you have any stories to share, about Master, for example?

The first night I met him it was in Paris. I had written down the address of an abhyasi in Paris to stay with, but somehow it got lost – and my flight was delayed so I arrived later than expected. I should have felt worried and I was in trouble but somehow I wasn't worried. I felt so calm inside, taken care of. Somehow I knew I was going to see Master and everything was fine. The only address I had (I didn't realize at the time) was where Master was staying, so I went there. There were many, many people waiting outside. I told them I was new so they let me in. He was watching a film and [was] surrounded by many abhyasis all around. I was too shy to introduce myself, so I sat down on the floor. Then I felt him coming into my heart and asking me, "Hello, how are you? Why are you here? What do you want from me?" It was really like we were having a chat. And I told him, "Hello, Master. Thank you for inviting me here. I'm so happy to see you. I don't know why I'm here; you know it better than me."

The next day there was satsangh. I was a bit late so had to stay at the back – and during that satsangh, I felt as if we were getting married, you know? I could see a feast going on, and flowers everywhere. I was dressed in this Indian way and it was really as if we were getting married. After that, there was a preceptor who introduced him to me saying, "Master, this is a new abhyasi. You've never met her." And he said, "Are you sure? Are you sure we've never met?" So he knew…

I have another story. I have a twin sister and my relationship with her has always been very difficult. I was the first to be born but was smallest; it seems she has always been very angry with me. I went to study abroad in England but she stayed at home; maybe she was a little bit jealous, [feeling] competition, I don't know. But the relationship was always a little bit difficult – especially when I came back from London, she was all the time angry with me. She would shout at me, "I don't know what you mean! I don't know what you are saying! You are doing this wrong," things like that. Even when talking with the family around the dinner table she could be very tough. So, the first time I came to India, I felt a lot was going on [regarding personal development]. When I came back, she was cooking and I was trying to help her and she was again telling me off; but somehow I was not affected by that. I realized that her telling me off was her problem, not my problem. So that was very different because before I was always feeling guilty; when she would attack me, I would think or say, "Okay okay. I'm sorry, I'm sorry." But this time it didn't touch me; this thing of feeling guilty wasn't there anymore at all. So I said, "Why are you reacting like that? I'm only trying to help you!" and she was totally shocked. [Since] then, our relationship has changed a lot and now it's much better. It's not completely solved, but at least she's not treating me as she was before, especially because she sees that it's not going to work.

I think that, when we change, all our surroundings have to change and this is an important point – that we are not alone. We are affecting our families, our friends, our colleagues.

Kim: Do you think it's important for abhyasis to marry abhyasis?

There is another story about that. I was going out with a boy and it was the kind of relationship where he was a strong man and I was a little girl. He was not an abhyasi. Suddenly, the relationship ended. I felt that this could have been my whole life [involved in a bullying situation] because I have this kind of character that I felt guilty, feeling I deserved their anger somehow, that I was never good enough... So he was acting a little bit like my sister, dominating me and telling me what to do – and I needed someone to tell me what to do because I didn't know what to do, you know? If I hadn't been an abhyasi, if I hadn't changed inside, I could've stayed with this guy and been in that relationship for my whole life. But I changed and the relationship ended, so another kind of person could come into my life. I'm now planning to get married, with an abhyasi. He wasn't an abhyasi when we started dating but he became curious and started. And somehow, that's important because the whole house becomes illuminated with this light. If one is meditating, they can still bring light into the house and into the family – but it can become bigger if the two of us are in the practice. Master says that, if two people are meditating, it's not one plus one but instead it is multiplied. It's easier then to augment this light, to create this [environment] not only in the house, but also in the whole family, in the world, in your society.

Kim: Will you be married in the mission, by Master?

Sure. I would love that. I would really love that.

Chapter 7

Stay the Course

Vicks

Indian, early 40's, male, self-employed

Preface: Vicks works for the mission part-time and I met him one day when processing some paperwork needed for my membership card. I spent some time in the office and did a little volunteer work while waiting for my business to be concluded. I enjoyed chatting with him and the two women helping. I liked his personality and sense of humor and wondered how someone who grew up in India and was educated through graduate school in the U.S.A. ended up working so much for the mission. I thought he might have some unique insights as someone who lives nearby and is part of life at this, the headquarters for the entire SRCM mission, an organization with ashrams and meditation centers in over 90 countries.

We meet, as prearranged, outside the library entrance, hoping some of the air-conditioned air inside will leak through to our hallway. We are in a breezeway overlooking the ashram grounds. A ceiling fan turns noisily overhead and we raise our voices slightly as we talk. Coming from generations interested in spirituality and mysticism, Vicks discusses growing up with a family guru and trying various approaches. He shares some of his feelings about the mission and about devout practice. He discusses the importance of a spiritual practice that allows an "unfolding" of oneself. He also says Sahaj Marg isn't for everybody. Critical of himself and, at times, of some aspects of the Mission, Vicks describes his personal goal, the pursuit of constant remembrance, *sahaja samadhi*.

Kim: Can you just tell me a little bit about your background, in particular, your formative experiences?   Then if you could go into how you became interested in spirituality, and why Sahaj Marg in particular. What's been your involvement in Sahaj Marg?

Actually, spiritually, I think my family back to my grandfathers on both my mother's and father's side, and even beyond before that, there have been many people interested in spirituality and mysticism to a very serious extent. My mother's uncle became a *sanyasi* (monk) in Rishikesh [a city known as the gateway to the Garhwal Himalayas, along the Ganges]. So that was one influence. In the family, there have been a lot of people who have been interested. My mother's uncle was married to a very spiritual lady. Her father was in the Theosophical Society, and I remember they used to look after the local branch of the Theosophical Society in Kochi, Kerala. I mean, that was more of a general influence, not a specific thing.

I went to a school called Chinmaya Vidyalaya, which was started by Swami Chinmayananda. And we had to do Geeta (Gita – both spellings are OK) classes every week or so. I was there for 12 years, so basically, 1st grade to 12th grade. But even in school when they talk about spirituality, to a certain extent I think it's more blind-faith rather than a real understanding. I think the comics we had, the Amar Chitra Katha, (this is a series of comics published by a person who wanted to get children of India interested in their mythology, their spirituality), we grew up, I mean I grew up, and my sister and our generation, we grew up with that. And that was probably the earliest exposure to spirituality. Because I remember reading about Dhruva who went off to the forest when he was a kid. But to shorten the whole story, that was a big influence. And then my parents actually were followers of a guru in Karnataka, originally from Kerala, north Kerala, very close to the border. They both were initiated. It was in some sense very similar to Sahaj Marg but a lot more rituals. Or I should say not rituals, but they would do the ritual saying, "This is the inner (esoteric) meaning of the

rituals." It is more difficult than sitting down and meditating –
and more expensive, by way of paying for the rituals.

So they [my parents] were followers of that guru. That was
while I was growing up. Then when I went to college, there was
the library, and I seemed to have spent more time reading about
Ramakrishna than my college books. So Ramakrishna
Paramhamsa and his experiences, especially spiritual experiences,
were quite interesting. A couple of my friends went into the
Hare Krishna group, and they got their heads shaved and all that
thing (except for a tuft at the back of the head). But it didn't
ring a bell for me.

After that, I went to the U.S.A. Until then, I had done a little
bit of practice, but not meditation – because I thought
meditation was something very difficult. It was only when I
started reading J. Krishnamurti (see references and resources)
that my idea of what meditation is changed. I was reading his
commentaries on living and the significance of life. That was in
the U.S., and I think that the place where I was working, the
Mission (SRCM) used to have open houses every year – and
one of the preceptors, her husband was working in the same
company. I used to get the emails sent to the company's India
mailing list about the open houses every year. I visited a friend,
and he had the book My Master (Rajagopalachari, 1989) and I
read that. I had been planning to start. I mean, I was reading
and I really wanted to start doing something so I joined Sahaj
Marg there and took three sittings. I think within a month or a
few weeks after that, I went for a retreat, a weekend (two-day)
gathering. It was quite nice.

Kim: As soon as you had the sittings, could you feel something going on?

Not particularly. In fact, for the first maybe three or four years,
it was a very boring experience. I mean, the thing that struck me
was actually Babuji's writing and his depth, or – I don't know if
depth is the right word – his range. He was talking about

infinity. At that time, I had little knowledge. The scriptures are very, you know, <u>Vedanta</u> especially, very voluminous. And you start, and they all kind of link with each other. You start here, and you end up going a lot of other places. And you don't know how to find your way back. It's a little bit like Master's speeches (chuckles).

Kim: He always seems to tie them up, though. It's funny how he brings it back somehow.

He is better these days (laughing). Earlier it would take him a few days to get back to the original point. So, yes. Samskara theory was very simple, very useful, but very difficult to follow (practice). And then you get to the point where you have reduced this to nothingness, or, as Babuji put it: "Reality is a dreary wasteland." So I mean, I did have certain experiences outside of meditation. Meditation itself was, you know... I was aware of things happening. There must have been something going on internally, I'm guessing, because I continued even after some not-very-pleasant incidents. My wife actually dropped out because of one of those, but I continued.

I used to go for these gatherings fairly religiously, actually. They used to take place every two to three months, so I met a lot of people. There was a person from L.A. who was very dedicated and still is. He was a big sort of an inspiration in terms of how he led his life. So, yes, I continued. Then, in 2004, we returned to India.

Kim: Did you expect to come here to Chennai and Manapakkam? I mean, how did that happen?

The idea was to return to India. I was very serious about coming and doing work for the mission and being with Master and all that.

Kim: What made you make that decision? I find that a really amazing thing, to just sort of say, "OK, I'm going to give my life to the mission."

No. In a very real sense, I have seen my mother and her family lead a dedicated spiritual life. And my father was actually a Communist party member. But in India, they don't throw away spirituality just because they're Communists. So he had also taken initiation, and he never stopped anything he used to do. I think he started going to temples again after he was close to retirement. But what I am trying to say, I think it's due to the Indian culture where people (in a Mission) help each other. You know when the guru comes, everybody gets together and puts up visitors in their houses. I already had a lot of experience with that growing up. There is a shared feeling of brotherhood. My family's previous guru was a lady, and they called her Amma, "mother." So we say everybody is "mother's children," and not in a scary way – in a really affectionate, loving sort of way.

Kim: Do you work full-time for the mission now?

Not any longer. I mean, I used to because initially it was necessary. The membership department here was giving out ID cards but the cards were not kept properly. And Chennai, for some reason, didn't have too many IT people. When I came, I think volunteers were coming once a week or twice a week. Later on, when they made these ID cards compulsory for coming into the ashram, we extended to every day, maybe an hour or two, so that we could give their cards faster. So that's how I started. It took a long time before people started coming and working every day but now I think it's settled down. The staff is getting paid and there are a few volunteers coming every day.

Kim: Do you feel that being an abhyasi has changed you in any way?

Yes, absolutely. In any spiritual practice, not just this one, if you go deep into yourself (mentally especially), psychologically you start understanding the things that drive you. You find you are inadvertently behaving in particular ways. By the way, in India, you can't really be out of society. You could just be walking on the road and 50 things would come at you on a daily basis. So it's not like living in the U.S. where you could be in your apartment for weeks at a time and nobody would know what was going on, or even care, for that matter.

India is that way very good for *bhog*, impressions – for a lot of things to come out. I have seen that – the way people drive, the way I drive, all that has changed over time. And being close to the family… I don't know how it would have been if we had stayed in the U.S.A. Definitely, following a spiritual practice does make a huge difference in understanding yourself, and in some ways being able to choose your reaction to situations. Not unconsciously reacting, but consciously responding to what is going on. There is a certain detachment that happens.

I mean, in Sahaj Marg, my take is that it is very effective in accelerating the bhog, accelerating the effects of it (especially) if you come to the ashram and attend satsangh every day regularly for a week. I notice over the last 12 to 13 years that I have been practicing that my sensitivity increases and the situations that I'm put into keep getting deeper. Even a simple thing like going to the bhandara – you'll volunteer, you will get involved in so many different things in three days, and you find that there is a sense that everything that happens is for a reason, or every event that takes place has got some significance. I might not be able to explain it very clearly, but you find out that things happen (for a reason). And if you have a day where nothing happens, that also has a reason.

Kim: Would you have any advice for someone who is just starting to think about spirituality?

I have difficulty giving advice. The very first couple of years, I was friends with a preceptor and she was saying, "So, how come you don't talk about this with your friends, family, whatever?" I said, "I don't know what it is I'm getting. I can't articulate or express what it is that is happening." I can do it now; but then, I couldn't. I also found that, if you get into spirituality, after a while it tends to become all-consuming and that is both good and bad. So I can't say that everybody is going to have a pleasant experience. It is something to try out. Well, let's say you want to learn skiing, or you want to go scuba diving. In that sense, it is like adding another experience or adding another sense organ to your life. But that sense organ, you know, sort of dominates after a while. That is the only thing that is important. I would say that, for the sake of curiosity, if somebody told you there was an amusement ride, you should try it out because everybody is talking about it.

I was reading a book in the library just before you came. A Buddhist monk from New York was saying what happens is, people get into spirituality and they worry about doing the meditation properly and doing it better than the other person does. Is this deeper? Why am I not going up? Why am I not going down, left, right, whatever. He says you should be able to treat it as a hobby, in the sense that a hobby is not something that you do because you feel pressured to do it. You do meditation, you don't do meditation. You go for a walk instead of meditation. A lot of things, I think, happen naturally. I would say that if you are interested in spirituality, it will happen naturally. You can try it out and see if you like it. But it is not something that you should be forced or should feel forced into doing. Some people start, and then they feel forced to continue in whatever they are doing, because they think something is going to happen. But as Master once said, "Spirituality is every human being's birthright." It should not be that somebody does it for peace of mind or because they want excitement or they want to have visions or things like that. That may or may not happen. It is an extension of your personality, which will happen whether you want it to happen or not. There are really no abhyasis or non-abhyasis. Everybody is a potential abhyasi.

So you shouldn't treat somebody as, this guy is part of the group, or this guy is not part of the group – and that takes a lot of doing. So advice? Not really. I would say that you should try it out because there is definitely something which is not mumbo-jumbo. It's not anything secret or hidden. There is a natural unfolding of yourself. Try it out for that reason, because you are curious. If you want to do it for other reasons, by all means, you can try it out. But it may or may not give you what you want, especially Sahaj Marg. The way I think of Sahaj Marg, it's like beating your head against the wall. It feels so good when you stop (laughing). So when things keep happening, after a while you are forced to adjust and expand yourself.

Kim: So is your goal liberation?

No, I'm interested in *sahaja samadhi* [total external awareness with total inner emptiness or absorption; see glossary]. That is this idea that you're leading your normal life, whatever your life is, but in the sense of what Babuji said, you are in constant remembrance, you are not creating more samskaras. Things are just happening by themselves.

Kim: We are in kind of serious times on our planet Earth. Do you see Sahaj Marg as a social movement, as a way to improve our world and help people be better?

At one point, I had a lot of problems with fellow abhyasis in Sahaj Marg and I had got to the point where I left. I don't know if "left" was the right word, but I did go and meet a few other people because I felt that I wasn't getting the support I expected from the preceptors [or from] the Master. In terms of comparison with other movements and, just being outside Sahaj Marg I realized that, in Sahaj Marg, if you accept the changes that are going on inside you, you tend to become more satisfied with less. I think Babuji said "more and more of less and less." In that sense, your needs, when they are reduced, your load (on the planet) or your rate of usage of resources of the planet also comes down. Yes, you can go first class, you can go business class, you can go economy. It depends. Somebody I know who says he can walk, he is really okay walking. Taking a bike, going by auto, taking a bus, you know, and taking a taxi [are] all different levels of resource usage. If you get to the point where, maybe not consciously but unconsciously, we are reducing our load on the planet, Sahaj Marg does help. If nothing else, sitting for 2 ½ hours a day not hurting anybody else is a load off planet Earth (laughing).

Kim: I love your sense of humor.

The Master, when people ask, "Why do you have all these cultural programs?" says, "It's a harmless thing. It keeps them sitting in one place." (laughter)

Kim: Do you have any particular memories, either funny, poignant, tragic, humorous?

With Master, every time I have met him, it's always been a shock. I completely agree that his focus is only on getting abhyasis to move forward spiritually. Once I was introduced to him, and then he said, "Are you an abhyasi?" Three of us said, "Yes, Master!" but then I realized I wasn't doing the abhyas (daily practice), so he was right to ask. But it took – even after that – it took a long time for me to start doing the daily meditation, the cleaning and all that stuff. So I think his focus is always there on what he thinks is needed [for my spiritual progress].

Kim: Do you have any comments on how the mission and Sahaj Marg in general has changed over time and what is coming up for the future?

I see, especially in the Manapakkam ashram, I see a lot of money being spent. Instead of using less resources, they seem to be using more, and that's a change. For example, in a 2004 bhandara, I was looking for a place to charge my phone because I had to call somebody. And people were getting upset (at my usage/waste of electricity). The last few years, there have been chargers [available at bhandaras]. So it's a change, but it is also a conscious decision that had to be made to match abhyasis and society. For example, the canteen is doing more and more, the menu is growing larger and larger – and that is simply because abhyasis are not willing to accept what is being given in the kitchen. As Babuji said, "I give simple food for the body and divine food for the soul." How many people are willing to accept that?

So I don't know. The interesting thing from being in the membership department, I see that people who join and then dropped out, they come back. Some of them come back two or three times and finally stay. It is not everybody who can enjoy or relish a practice which is so internalized. So you have to, to some extent, love each other, because what you see is basically inside you. If you are not basically a – what should I say – a person who is okay with herself, then you will have quite a bit of trouble. As things come out, if you stay the course, then yes, you will become much more settled, more peaceful. But it is important to accept that fate – that things will get better, or they are getting better. Thank you.

Chapter 8

Salaam

Yasman

Iranian now living in the U.S.A.
Farsi as L1, female, late 30's, physical therapist

Preface: I meet Yasman one day outside the gate to Chariji's (Master's) cottage. She is often there when not meditating or running errands. She likes nothing better than to be near Master when in India. We need to meet partly to arrange for her to pick up some clothing she left last time she was in India. She comes several times a year, often enough to leave clothes behind for the next visit. She has stored her clothes in the bedroom I am borrowing so we arrange to meet and I help get her clothes down from overhead storage. I like Yasman's feisty personality and am interested in her background, coming from Iran with a Muslim heritage. I find she is a dynamo in a small, strong body. I appreciate her frankness and insights as I get to know her over the next few days as we attend a city outing together and share a pizza. We meet in the kitchen in a home where she is house-sitting, only a few blocks from the back gate of the ashram. Construction seems to be taking place on all sides as we try to find a quiet setting for our meeting.

In this interview, Yasman shares her own rocky start in spirituality and the path she took as a young woman, until finally, she became regular in her practice. She describes her attempts to emigrate from Iran, her first two trips to India, meeting Master, and the special attention and coincidences brought to her life as a consequence. She offers solid advice to newcomers to spirituality, including an awareness that one must work hard, accept hardships, be responsible, and bring one's whole heart to the practice. Reflecting on her challenges over the years, including physical trauma and a broken marriage, Yasman encourages us to work on changing ourselves. She also warns us that involvement in spirituality does not mean an end to suffering.

Kim: Can you tell me about your background?

I grew up in Iran. When I was 27, I moved to Canada. I stayed there for almost five years then I moved to Seattle. Later I moved to the Bay area, close to San Francisco. Now I live in L.A., Los Angeles.

Kim: Was it hard to get out of Iran?

Very, very, very hard. That was one of the toughest things. Because of the political situation in Iran, it was very difficult to get even a visitor visa to visit other countries. My sister had her baby overseas and I couldn't even go visit her.

Kim: How did you become involved in Sahaj Marg?

I was introduced to Sahaj Marg ten years ago, through a friend. Before Sahaj Marg, I practiced a couple of different systems, all meditation-based. And I did some yoga, but it was never the main thing. Since I was very, very young – I can't even remember how old I was, but I was very young - I had this feeling inside me that I had everything necessary to be happy but I was not happy. I had a good family and I was going to a good school. Everything was normal, but I was not happy. Even when I was a teenager, something was missing but I didn't know what it was. Nobody around me was practicing meditation, or ever talked about these kinds of things. I didn't know what it was, but I was missing something big and I was somehow restless.

Kim: Was your family religious?

No but they have faith. We had that faith in the family with God and all that kind of stuff. I grew up in Iran where most people are Muslims. My family is Muslim, but we are not fundamentalist. If you live in Iran, when you go outside in the street you have to wear covers. But inside the house, amongst our family, we could go to family parties and do everything that people from other parts of the world do.

My mother is a Persian literature teacher, so there was a lot of talk of Rumi and Sufism and mysticism in my home. Nobody was practicing anything specific, but I was familiar with these ideas – like Rumi had a guru or *mourshed*. *Mourshed* is a word in Farsi for Master. So it was there, but I was never that involved. Neither was my mother. There was the literary point of view like Hafiz or like Saadi (see references and resources), different big poets of Iran that kind of marked the history in Iran and also in other places in the world. There was that kind of atmosphere, but there was no practical issue. I was praying the way Muslims pray, and fasting as the Muslims do, but that was about it. It was very much on the mild side of the religion. It was never a huge thing in my life. It was faith that was huge.

When I was about 18 or so, I had a friend who asked me if I wanted to try TM, Transcendental Meditation. It is a hefty bill to pay, and of course, when you're 18 you don't have much income. But I knew that I needed something and maybe this would help me. I was 17 when I lost my Dad. I was in grade 12, I lost my Dad, and I had to prepare for entrance exams for university.

In Iran, we have a free university system but there is a huge entrance exam. You graduate from high school in grade 12 and then you do a big entrance exam. Based on your score on that exam, you are matched for different fields of study in different universities. It's very competitive. So there was that pressure.

Also, I always had this kind of thing with my mother and we never were that close. She's great; she's a great woman. It's just her ways were different and everything was different now that we'd lost my Dad.

Kim: Sometimes personalities don't match very well.

Yeah. Anyways, that was my Master's gift later on. I realized she did her best. What she taught, it's the best, and that soothed me a lot later on in my life because I always thought that she didn't like me or she liked my brother and sister more... [silly] teenager years. I give credit to my Master that I could go through all of that. Anyway, this family friend of mine told me that there's a practice that he was doing. He said he had a very good teacher; there was no talk of a guru or anything. He told me to go and see him, and I went and started TM. And boy, oh boy, it was a different story. For me, it was not "wow" the first time that I did it because it took me a while to actually go deep. Once I started feeling this meditation - the business of meditation and going inside - it changed my life.

In TM, there is this funny thing that, at every grade, you have to go through different levels and you have to pay an extra fee to get the training for the next level. I understand, you are renting a place and I don't have a problem [helping to pay for upkeep]. But if this is love, that sat a little uncomfortable with me, the fact that I have to pay this teacher to teach me how to love, to get to the next level.

I wasn't great with my practice but it opened the whole world for me. Because of all the things I had gone through, I was depressed and needed a lot of help so I was going to this psych[ological] consultant. When I started, I wasn't on any medication, but the person that I was consulting said that I was at the point that I really needed more help than what they could give by just speaking [counseling]. So I had to take some medication, but I didn't want my family to know. Imagine the chaos. It was a tough time. I did go to the doctor, feeling skeptical. I was not well and I was skeptical about how much they knew about the brain; nobody knows much. With this medication, sometimes you have to be on it for three or four weeks, at least, until you know it is working for you.

They started me on a very common anti-depressant, but apparently, this was a bad thing for me because it made me even worse. Because I was feeling so bad, I thought maybe I had to continue for at least a month (to see the effects), but I was feeling worse and worse. After a month, I went back to the doctor and he asked why I didn't call him earlier! Then they gave me another medication and it started working.

I started TM at the same time. It was to me like I was introduced to life; it was like that. How big it was, because I was sick and I was depressed for a while, a couple of months. Yes, of course it was medication too, but it was like I realized the meaning of life. I didn't know anything much more than that I felt alive. I had been very, very depressed but soon, within six months, I didn't need to take medicine - and I was fine. It was like a miracle in my life.

The year I graduated was the year that I was going through all the nuances of being unwell. I didn't receive a good grade for the entrance exam so I had to take it again the next year. My score was good enough to be accepted to PT (Physical Therapy) school. At that time I had no clue what PT was; I wanted to be a doctor. At least it was the same field, and the pressure of university admission lifted. My sister was in medical school and I liked to help so I knew I wanted to be in the medical field. I was thinking of being a doctor, but it was not meant to be. I thank the universe because I love my job; I don't think any other job would give me the satisfaction of this job, especially the interactions. I've always liked to be with people and being in the helping business is the best gift of the universe for me.

So I got to PT school. At that time, I wasn't practicing TM as much, but I was well. I kind of felt that I understood the meaning of life. It's as if I was introduced to this world again.

After that, I was kind of looking. I went to some Sufis (and this is underground because it's not a widespread practice in Iran). Although this country [Iran] is famous for those Sufi teachings, because of the political system, it wasn't widespread. I did that, and nothing fit as much, but I was searching in different places. Meanwhile, I was also going to school. I graduated from PT school and wanted to leave Iran. It was my biggest mission in life that I leave Iran, which is not easy. So I applied to a couple of different places. I applied to go to Australia, England and Canada. Canada seemed to be the most feasible. The people with whom I was going to school were a year ahead of me and they all applied for Canada; within a year, they all got their immigration papers sorted out, which was great. I started working but the main focus was to somehow get out of Iran. I applied for immigration to Canada in December of 2000 but then, in 2001, [the terrorist attacks of] September 11 happened. There was a big block on immigration because the U.S.A. was blaming the Canadians. For four years, I was just waiting and not sure if I was going to get out. Nothing would go through. This was a huge struggle for me at the time. I couldn't settle down in Iran because I was always thinking that I was leaving. And those were my best years, my twenties. I was feeling miserable again because I was stuck. I had the money. I had a good family to support me – but I couldn't get out.

So meanwhile I travelled. I travelled mostly in the Middle East region and Turkey and Syria, around Dubai. I did not travel much outside of that region because nobody would grant a visa. Meanwhile, I was looking for different systems. I wasn't specifically looking for meditation but I was looking for something to which I could feel connected. I went on retreat for a practice called Vipassana (see references and resources section), which is very close to Sahaj Marg. They have a guru but I didn't even know what that meant. You go to this retreat for ten days and they train you to do their meditation. This idea of retreat is that you are in silence; you're avoiding your senses so it is easier to go inside.

Kim: You don't talk?

No. That's the idea. I was very stringent about sticking to the rules, until the last night when you're allowed to talk, so I started talking a lot. Everyone said that they didn't think that I would survive not talking, because I'm a talkative person, as you can see here. I was a seeker. And this was another one of those introductions that felt really good. In Vipassana, one thing that they were stressing, or at least so I understood at that time, was about the posture to sit and meditate, so like the lotus position to sit without your back supported. I had a lot of issues with my hips and my back even though I was young, and for whatever reason it was difficult for me. But I got it. I got the point that maybe I had to go through this hardship so then my body would be cooperative. But I had a hard time. Every time I would sit there was something uncomfortable with my body. And I'm not looking for comfort. I'm from an Eastern culture and it's not that everything has to be perfect. No, no, no. But it [discomfort] shouldn't disturb your state of connection.

So that was something that I was having a hard time with, but it is a very beautiful system. Beautiful. They do have a guru, his name is Goenka, and he lives in India. This is the closest system to the teaching of Buddha so it's very widespread, even in America. I know people that are practicing it. They have retreats that are free of charge because it's the business of love. I can get connected to that. When it's talking about love, I don't mind paying. But your actions and your words have to match and I found this one did.

I had just come back from that retreat and it was my close friend's wedding a couple of days later. Soon after his wedding, he was going to emigrate to Canada. He was one of the people that I knew from PT school and I was helping with the wedding preparations, going to his place to set things up. He was telling me about a friend of his who was crazy like me and went to India all the time. He didn't know what I was doing; he just knew I had recently been to a retreat, and he said I should talk to his friend. I said to my heart, "I just found this system and I'm practicing and I just have to do it a little bit to feel it, but okay. It doesn't matter. I can talk to the guy; it's fine." This guy was in the wedding party and we talked very briefly; I already had my mindset that I've already started this system (Vipassana) and I might as well give it some time. After that, I could try something else. We exchanged phone numbers but I never called him.

A couple of months later, I don't even remember how long it was, I received a call from the Sahaj Marg group. They said that they have introduction sessions if I wanted to come. I thought there was no harm in going to the introduction so I went and liked the people very much. But again, I wasn't thinking of starting anything and was still trying Vipassana. I went home and soon after, received a call. They said they had scheduled me for an introductory sitting if I wanted to come. This was the strangest thing because I'm always very mind-oriented. I have to know things before I do things. For whatever reason (divine plans?), I didn't say no. I went and started meditation at the end of May, 2003. I started meditation and meanwhile I'm still waiting for Canada.

Kim: And was that system different?

In Vipassana, I can't quite remember what we were meditating on. We didn't have a mantra or an object or anything, that I know. They were very chakra-oriented because their plan was to open this Crown Chakra.

So when I was introduced with Sahaj Marg, I wasn't that impressed. It wasn't anything new to me; it wasn't a new concept that you meditate and connect with your inner self. A month later I got my papers to immigrate to Canada. I looked at the date of the letter and it was the same date that I started Sahaj Marg. People say you shouldn't connect these things, but in my heart I thought there was a connection, because I was so desperate all those years. Anyway, I thought that, if I go abroad, I'm going to meet this man they are talking about, this Master they are talking about. I have a hard time accepting the idea of Master, which is funny being from an Eastern culture. I had a very difficult time with that. Am I not enough to do it by myself? Do I need a mediator between me and God?

But I knew I was moving abroad and it was going to be a chaotic couple of years in the beginning as I settled down there. I didn't think I would have time to do this kind of spiritual search again. I was feeling there was something good about it. A Master is very important in this system. I've got to know him.

So I went to Dubai the first time Master went to Dubai, in October of 2003, and I was introduced to him only four months after I took my first sittings. I happened to know one of the people in Dubai and they actually took me in and introduced me to him personally and we said "Hi" to each other, but I didn't feel anything special during that trip. I was surprised as to why people were crying when they saw him, or why everybody was rushing after him. I didn't have any special feeling or anything about him. But somehow, he's an attractive person. He's charismatic, even if you don't know anything about 'guru.'

There were a couple of things I remember from that first time, even though I wasn't speaking much English. [I just tried to catch] whatever I could remember, whatever I could get. One of the things that he was saying is that, if you are going to go up a mountain, you take this man as a guide, a mountain guide. You don't normally question him or his credentials. You take him as somebody who can take you up and knows the road. If you go to school and you have a professor in chemistry, you know that professor knows more about chemistry than you do. So, he said, just accept me as that, just as a teacher. I am your teacher, and nothing more. That's it. Another example he gave was to imagine you want to go from point A to point B and you can go many ways. You can bike or walk, have a car, ride a donkey. But he said, "I am like a plane for you guys. Get a ride from me. I am like that plane." So I had these things in mind and in my heart.

He goes there [to Dubai] a lot because he knows it's not easy for Iranians to leave Iran. He had two or three sessions with Iranians and, in one of the interactions, I will never forget his words. He said that, "If you want to see the lion, you have to see him in his field." Because he was born a Leo, his symbol is a lion. So I took that to heart and, soon after, took my first visit to see him.

It was a four-day seminar and, on the way coming back from Dubai, they were talking about being vegetarian. I had been in yoga for more than ten years and tried to become a vegetarian a couple of times. It was good for a week and then I couldn't. So I was sitting in the plane going back to Iran from Dubai and they served a meal and I could not look at that meat. Very simple. I didn't even try after that. During the first year, maybe I had two burgers because I had that craving, but that was it. I didn't even feel I needed it. End of story, I have been a vegetarian ever since. And it was never even a priority for me to become a vegetarian. I wish everything else was coming so easy for me.

It is October and I'm back in Iran. All of my paperwork for Canadian immigration is ready. I have done my medical and everything; I am just waiting for my visa to come. [And I decided] it wasn't enough. I didn't know this man enough, so in December I went to India. I went to India in December and end of the story. Again, nothing in particular happened. But, I don't know, he somehow connects you. I went from Iran to Calcutta waiting for Master to come there. I knew nothing, I knew nobody. I was just going there. Finally, the Master arrives. He's walking on the premises and I'm just standing there, not even close. I was standing on a curb and he passed by me. There were so many people around him I doubted he even saw me. (The funny things we doubt about a spiritual person.) He went past me, but then he turned back and said to me "salaam." He didn't know me; I didn't know him. But he said salaam to me, which means hello in Farsi (laughs). And he went. He just said salaam and he went.

I'm not getting this. I'm not even a particle in this world and nobody even knows me, and I don't know a single person there but then this guy turns to me and says "salaam." So, okay. That's good. That's okay, but I'm still kind of unsure about what's going on, what is happening. Is this the blessing of the universe happening to me? I don't know. My heart (or my mind) are still analytical.

So here comes another experience. He is selling tokens. Back then he used to do a lot of these things. He was in the canteen and was selling tokens. I'm a simple person; I gave money. I can't remember, I gave 500 rupees but then he gave me just one token [valued at] 100 rupees. Of course, I'm not going to go back and ask where are the rest of my tokens. So my mind goes on and on. Why is he doing this? I'm on a limited budget. It costs a lot to come here. What is going on? And I was pissed off. So I put this as a little test for him. I need to get the rest of my 400 by the end of my trip. If not, I'm out of here. This guy is just looking for money, and I didn't know the meaning of donation. I knew the meaning of donation but I didn't know that it was a blessing to get a token from his hand. All these things, I know nothing; I'm just thinking of the 400 rupees that I'm missing. I've just come from Iran, I don't have much, and all of that.

So I happened to volunteer in the bookstore. One day, we are counting the money and, at the end of the day, I have 400 rupees extra, out of I don't know where. I just don't know where (laughter). That's good! There's my test and he passed the test for that 400 rupees. So that was another good sign.

There was an inauguration of another ashram in Ongole. I followed along and we found a place to sleep. That day I called home to Iran and my mother told me that the Canadian embassy had called and my visa had arrived, the visa I had been waiting for over four years. But now [I had] another problem. I knew nobody in Canada. What am I supposed to do? Where should I go? Everybody was saying that I had to ask Master but... He's a Master of other things; he's not a Master of these things, [I'm thinking]. This is my life; I have to take care of it myself. But they said I should ask him. I knew nothing because my English was limited. I hadn't been in Sahaj Marg long, not even six months. I knew that, when I was in his presence, I could not speak (it had happened a lot of times). He said salaam to me and I couldn't even say salaam back. So I wrote on a little piece of paper that I am going to emigrate to Canada and I don't know where to go because I don't know anybody in Canada.

I kept the paper with me at the Ongole ashram. It was one of the nights that he came out and sat outside of his cottage. Maybe 200 people were just sitting around and it was very informal. There was a beautiful full moon and no conversation. I was three or four rows back and there were a lot of people – not like now when I try to be in the front row (laughs). He was sitting a distance in front of us. Every now and then somebody would say something, but it was mostly silent. Then, out of the blue, out of all those people, he summoned with his finger, saying to come here. I'm just sitting there; I didn't think [he meant] me. Somebody beside me stood up and he said, "No, no, no. You." Somebody behind me stood up and he said, "No, you." and then I realized he was talking to me. For a couple of days I had carried this letter with me explaining that I am going to go to Canada. I didn't go to him; he asked me to go. So I went and stood beside him but I can't speak. He talks to me; I can't even remember what he was telling me. So I just give him the letter. He opened the letter and read that funny little note I wrote him, not even like an official nice letter. "Oh, you are going to Canada. That's very nice." And then my question was where to go. "Oh, you go to B.C." And people beside me said, "Oh, Master. She should go to Toronto. So and so is in Toronto." "She should go to Calgary." "No, I think B.C. is the best for you," he said.

I didn't think this was anything that stood out, but afterwards people were saying, "You are lucky. Master normally doesn't say these things." He blesses everybody but normally doesn't give specific advice to people.

And I said okay, fine. I'm telling you because he knew my mind, my funny mind. I went to say bye the last day and we're coming out of his cottage. Everybody is out [but then] one of the people who work for him comes and calls me, "You, you Iranian one come. Master wants to have dinner with you." I had no idea what a blessing it is to have dinner with Master. I go and silently have my dinner, saying nothing very peacefully and coming out. That's it. That was my first trip from India. Departing, I had a 24-hour train trip to Mumbai, then my flight from Mumbai to Iran. I was feeling very good and high because I was excited about going to Canada.

Kim: Your dreams were coming true.

Exactly. But the story doesn't stop there. On the train, I was asking people how to get from the train station to the airport and this lady who is sitting beside me says she doesn't know but she has friends coming to pick her up who are locals and I could ask them. We arrive at six in the morning and my flight is at two in the afternoon. Her friend came and I asked how to get to the airport. The guy said he was going to the airport at ten in the morning to pick up some people and he would take me. This is the first time I had met him and he invited me to come to his house, saying we can have food and then he can take me to the airport. I don't know this guy at all. He was working for the embassy of Malaysia or Singapore or someplace, I can't remember. He told me that he and his children travel all the time and he is happy to help me. I was feeling uncomfortable and I said no. But he came with his wife and, since she was there, I felt safe – and this lady passenger I was talking to was also with them. So they take me to their home and their maids serve me food but the food is non-vegetarian. I told them that I could not eat the food, and the lady of the house personally went and prepared a vegetarian meal for me, for somebody that they hadn't even seen before!

They gave me a room and I took a shower and refreshed before they took me to the airport. Funny enough, that day there was something happening, some sort of riot. Nobody could stop right in front of the airport. Even if you went in a taxi, they would drop you a lot further away, so you had to walk. But this guy was from an embassy so he had a special car, like special permission, so they took me right to the gate. Before I knew it, I'm sitting in a plane and going back to Iran. So that was my first trip to India.

Two months later, I moved to Canada. Sadly enough, I didn't come back [to India] for 6 years. I was so busy taking care of my life and getting things sorted out. I went to school and did a Master's degree - and of course, I had to learn English better. Every now and then, I was connected to Sahaj Marg but I wasn't doing my practice. I was going for satsangh maybe once a month and maybe, once in a blue moon, I would sit for my meditation and my cleaning. But inside, I felt connected. There was no contact; I wasn't even writing emails [to Master]. The abhyasi groups were quiet, minding their business. (Not that I expected anybody to take care of anybody but just kind of encouraging you to come and to do this and to do that). All in all, it was very quiet... which means that you come whenever you feel you want to. It was a strange thing to me because I'm from a different culture and, in the beginning, it was a big cultural difference. I went to Victoria, B.C., which is a small town and rather isolated, a very small abhyasi group. It happened that the prefect's house was only a 10-minute walk from my house, but I was going there very seldom. She was accommodating to me, but I was somewhere else.

Six years later, at the beginning of 2009, I moved to the U.S.A. I was wondering what I should do, where I should go. I'd been to B.C., where he told me to go when I moved to Canada, but I always wanted to go to the U.S. because I have family there – but I wasn't sure if I should do that. I finally decided to go, went to Seattle and settled, earning an income with my PT license. I decided it was about time for me to go back to India so I went in December 2009 after six years. I don't know what I was thinking, not going for so many years. I came back [to India] and it was a huge reminder of what I was missing. This was my goal, my life. [After that trip], I started becoming regular in the practice and I started going two to three times a year to India. A whole lot of things happened right after that, but that was the beginning of this journey to truly start Sahaj Marg.

As I said, I was always looking for something. Even when I was very young, not even in my teenage years, maybe nine or ten, I would sit in silence. I was always turning off the light and sitting in silence. I said I was having a conversation with God. I didn't know I was meditating [but] maybe I was. I don't know what I was doing; I have no clue, but I had to bring meaning to my life. I think I was very restless and unhappy, despite a good life. I had everything that a teenage girl may want, except that I was in Iran. I have a good family and financially we were all good. It wasn't that I was desperate for anything. I had almost everything that I needed for a good life, materially and all that.

But something was missing big time, and that was my search of the soul, which I couldn't even put into words. My soul was searching for something, or my heart was looking for something. I had no clue what I was missing. That's basically it. At a very young age I knew there was something else to this than just going to work and going to school [but] I didn't know what.

Kim: Do you feel that Sahaj Marg has changed you?

Oh my God! (laughter) That's the whole business of this Sahaj Marg, it's about change. It changes the approach of how you live life, how you look at things. A lot of times, it doesn't come easy, I have to add. It is not an easy journey.

You think, once you start meditating, everything has to be peaceful and grateful and Master is going to give you all good things. No, 'ain't happening.' If anybody was looking for that, you probably would be disappointed with this system. The gist and the understanding - at least from what I know right now, which is very limited understanding - is that somehow we have to go through certain things to become purer and to get closer to our source. Because we have a Master who is there to support us and to help us, he's not going to let us fall.

I always felt, even before starting Sahaj Marg, something about this universe is, I'm always protected. I had this faith - and it didn't come from religion, because religion has a lot of fear in it - I have this faith that, no matter what, I have help, I have somebody. Not like the Christian guardian angel, I never believed in any specific entity to take care of me. I thought that this whole system would take care of me. Now I'm not alone. I may be sometimes lonely, feel lonely, but I am not left alone. I may feel emotional or whatever – but I still feel I am protected, and that's an amazing feeling on its own, more so in the past couple years. After I go through certain hardships, I feel I must have gone through that for a reason [even if] I absolutely have no clue what is that reason. If the reason comes to me, perfect.

If it doesn't come to me, again perfect, because I know I am protected and there is a very good reason that I have to go through this hardship. I'm hoping and praying that I cooperate with this, that I don't go against the flow of nature.

That's my only thing that I'm still sometimes feeling or kind of stumbling with - am I really following, am I really not fighting it? I used to fight a lot. My nature was, I had something in mind, oh *mama mía* – the world comes between me and the thing that I think is right for me - I just go; I was like that. Again, I guess it's his grace to teach me that you've got to go with the flow. I will tell you the example some sister told me; it's exactly me. She said, imagine this is the flow of water and there is a stone in this water. You are the one, instead of going around this stone, you want to drill that stone and go through that stone. It's absolutely true. I didn't know the secret of nature. These are the secrets, or the rules of nature, that I'm understanding little by little by the teaching of the system, by the teaching of Master.

Kim: What's the biggest lesson or burden you have had to endure?

The past four, almost five years of my life, have been one thing after another. I thought I was settled so I could move on and have a nice peaceful life and a family and all that. But somehow, one thing after another came that really disturbed my life. For example, after my first trip to India I had a big car accident. I had never been in a car accident before that. Somehow I missed a stop sign and the other guy was coming very fast in a residential area. So I hit him; of course, my fault. That was just the week after I came back from India. If you would have looked at the two cars, you would think the two drivers would be dead, finished. My airbag blew, the radiator blew, so all the hot water was coming in... but somehow, I got out of that car with not even a scratch. It took me a minute to realize I was still there; it was a big shock. So I come out and I'm running to know what happened to this other person and I see somebody, like he was walking and he was on the phone, of course calling 911 emergency assistance.

The other driver's car was thrown into a neighbor's yard. Later I learned that a lady was working in her garden about the time this car was thrown into that garden. She went inside to grab a cup of water right at that time. (If she hadn't gone inside, she would have been hurt seriously).

Kim: I'm glad you mentioned that because it seems that people think they can sort of leave everything in the hands of the Master and everything will be fine. But people haven't really talked about some of the pains and hardships some of them have to go through. People can get the wrong impression.

No. It doesn't mean that he's going to interfere. He always says - which it took me a while to understand - that you have to fulfill nature's plan for your creation. From my understanding, that's what he says. I don't know what nature's plan is for me. Nature's plan is, I cooperate with nature and, whatever comes my way, I accept; I surrender. Surrender doesn't mean I'll be a passive person. I don't go to work and say Master will help me, nuh-uh. You've got to take care of your responsibilities. It is your first duty. You have to take care of your family. You've got to take care of your financial responsibilities. You've got to take care of your life fully and completely, 100%. This is your responsibility; it is nobody else's responsibility. If I go to my Master and tell him I'm poor and need money, it's my problem. In this system, I take care of my responsibilities. I do my best. My Master worked all his life. He worked, he retired and now he's having a retired life but he's still working day and night for us now. He worked like a normal person, took care of his family, did all the [usual] things – this Master and other Masters of Sahaj Marg. Probably the other Masters, the great Masters of the universe, they all did the same things.

The trick here is that, number one, don't expect anything. Don't expect that, when you come here, it's going to be all nice and beautiful. A lot of us have done, including myself. So this was again a big shock. Now that I'm starting to be sincere, I'm starting to [understand] why this has to happen.

A lot of other experiences happened to me. I'm a physical therapist, so you work with your body; you are like a worker with your body. If your body is out of commission, you are out of commission. Two and half years ago, I had a very, very severe back injury so I couldn't work. It threw my back off and I couldn't even stand; I couldn't sit, I couldn't lie [down], everything was painful. Of course, my great career was ruined and what the hell was I supposed to do? Again [this was] a blessing in disguise because I had to go through a lot of therapy. Therefore, I got to know and to do a lot of alternative therapies which are an asset for me now. I was always kind of interested, but I was trained as a conventional physical therapist in the Western medicine system; that's what I do. So this helped me learn a lot about alternative treatments. I did visceral manipulation and craniosacral therapy, for example. I got to know a lot about all these alternative [treatments] that exist in this beautiful world of ours. I'm not an expert on them but at least I'm familiar. I got actual training for some and, for others, I can refer people to other specialists. So again, it was a blessing in disguise. There is a reason for this to happen to you, so just move on. Move on and go with the flow.

The biggest experience I had was that I had a short marriage. It didn't go the way I was thinking marriage and a relationship were supposed to go. We are separated now and I've been suffering for the past year and half about it but, again, I cannot do anything. It is out of my control. All I can do is to work on and change myself. I cannot do anything else in this world. The teaching of my Master is that, when you change yourself, it's like you are changing a piece of the puzzle, the world puzzle – so you are changing the world. But we are not changing the world, we are changing ourselves. Our work is to change ourselves and then, as a consequence, other things happen.

Kim: Do you think Sahaj Marg has a role to play in the future as a force of change, a force of social change?

Oh my God, of course! Even the Master of this system says I'm not going to change the world. It will change by the effect of every person changing. If my Master is saying that, if this guy that I'm accepting as my Master, as my guide, is saying that then I'm not going to change the world. But I think everybody who's really sincerely doing the practice from their heart, they realize how much change it brings to their life, so it must somehow spread to people with whom you associate. You don't want to go and ask people to come and join but people will come and talk to you about it. Whether they join or not, that is beside [the point]. But they will see that there is something different that they don't see elsewhere, or they don't see every day in a busy material life.

I live in L.A. and you can imagine how material life can be there. However, within the same community live a whole lot of beautiful souls. Everybody in this world is looking, because we are all far from our source.

Kim: What advice would you have for somebody who is just starting to look around?

Just really try it. Give it a try full-heartedly. Start doing your practice, if Sahaj Marg is the one that you're choosing, and give it some time. Very, very, very few people have an immediate connection with the system, with the Master, within their heart, but give it time. I am telling you, this is the miracle of Sahaj Marg; it gets you connected to the universe. You are good and comfortable with you - not good, but you have got to know yourself (a little bit but piece-by-piece). Again, circumstances come, situations come, and you get to know yourself more. You get your dark side, you get your good side, you get your happy side - all the sides - but just hang in there and sincerely do your practice.

You ask nature, you ask the universe, they're all the same - my Master is the representative of the universe for me. One of the biggest things that helped me is the prayer at bedtime. From the heart, if there is anything that bothers you, if there is anything in your behavior you want to change, pray. For example, I had a lot of issues with reaction, with my anger, a lot of issues with connections, even with myself. So in my bedtime prayer, I sincerely asked from my heart, feeling desperate. "I am trying all I can do but I am desperate. I need your help. This universe can help me. This is my request. This is my plea to you. Help me." Then you leave it, you don't go back. You have this faith that the universe or Master (or whomever you want to call it) will listen and will somehow respond. This is exactly what I have been finding to be a very powerful tool we have.

A beauty of this system is that it is full of tools but you don't need to change your practice. I am doing the same thing I was doing 10 years ago, as are people who have been in this system for 40 years - so the practice is the same - but what you do, what you feel, what you experience is different. Don't look for experiences. Don't compare, that's the biggest thing. Comparison can really bring us down. Every person has his own experience with the Master, with the system.

Even for me, after so many years, I may not have an encounter with my [physical] Master but I can encounter his essence, and the world or universe that he introduced to me. So, even if I don't have a physical encounter with him, it doesn't matter because the connection is somewhere else. There are so many of us and he's an old Master, physically; but don't let this physical form deceive you. This is way beyond that physical form, and his essence is the one that you're trying to connect to, not his physical form. Our part is to do our work. If you are going to start this system, start it. Do it. Give it some time. And then you will see for yourself. If within six months, if within a year, you don't feel any connection, you don't feel any change, you don't feel anything, then maybe you have to go and look for something else. That's okay. You should give it all your heart, all your being, or else you cannot judge it. Just hang in there. Thank you very much.

Chapter 9

Non-Doing Doing

Martin

Raised in the U.K., but now living in India, male, 60's, a multi-tasker, farmer, taxi services, apartment manager and lens crafter (eyeglasses)

Preface: I can't wait to interview Martin. He is among the first abhyasis I met in India because he has a business giving people rides to and from the airport. We'd enjoyed chatting, me picking his brain about ashram life and happenings, him telling me about the book he is writing, and other occasions when he helped with transportation, phone cards or computer supplies. He is a well-respected and well-known figure around the ashram, which is odd because Martin seems somewhat shy at times. Lean and lanky, with white hair and eyes swimming behind thick glasses, he is irreverent, self-deprecating, and oh-so-human. We settle into the living room at his apartment, located directly across the road from the ashram main entrance, and are ready to begin. We settle in for a long story of a young man's longing and discovery. We can also experience a little of the hippy revolution of the sixties in this story.

Martin left Europe for India as a young man because he could find no value in status, materialism or the traditional life into which he was being "directed." He explores truly being in the moment and "non-doing doing" as he describes his first meeting with Babuji, founder of the Shri Ram Chandra Mission and precursor to Chariji, then the current living Master (see references and resources). During years of travel and searching, he explains how his personal goals of mergence with the Divine have transformed. He eloquently expresses his hopes for humanity in both the near and distant future. Martin's story may give you pause for reflection – and maybe make you laugh out loud – or perhaps cry. For more details as to Martin's story, make sure to read his book (see Worthy, M. in references and resources).

Kim: I'm curious about your upbringing and background. Can you talk a little about that and how you became interested in meditation?

I was born into a middle-class, suburban, Christian family (Protestant or Church of England schooling) and then, at the age of about 16 (this was during the mid-60s, the emergence of rock and roll and the hippies, with changes afoot), I moved away from religion and the mainstream middle-class/suburban behavior patterns of my schoolmates. At the age of 22, I dropped out of university and came to India for the first time. My interest was in the Orient, the exotic, the alternative, the fact that it was different from my background.

One of my friends used to fly off to exotic destinations at weekends (to Morocco, to Tel Aviv). His family worked for one of the airlines and could get flights dirt cheap, and he'd always come back with amazing stories. He would meet like travelers on the road, give them his address, and they'd turn up to stop by his flat to crash. So in 1972, I tried it out, hitchhiking to Istanbul and back and getting a feel for the big, open road. The next year, 1973, I got together enough money and set off on a bigger voyage. First I went to Europe and then to India and back, nearly two years "on the road."

At that time, I was looking to get away from the middle-class suburban material security thing that society was trying to push me in to. I didn't really know what I was looking for – I had no particular destination when I set off. So, as a kickoff, I went to see two dear friends, one in Denmark and another in Stuttgart, Germany. Then I went down alongside the Adriatic and on to Istanbul, then into Iran and Afghanistan. Afghanistan was great, the first truly Eastern or Oriental place I had visited. However, I could only get a one-month visa so I quickly had to move on to Pakistan, where I felt too much tension to dally. Both politics and Islamic sectarianism made me feel insecure so I proceeded into India. Everything changed when I entered the border into India; the feeling was one of being at home. I spent a year and a half in India at that time, in the mountains, in the valleys, in the fields of Punjab – several places but all in the top northwestern corner of the country.

That first trip, I set off with £200 and, when I got back to England nearly 2 years later, I had £40 left. I spent maybe twenty nights in total during the two years in hotels. For six months, I lived in a teashop sleeping on the tables, doing a bit of work but not earning a salary, just having food and being – same as on the farm where I lived for some months. I was trying to break the bonds of what everyone else was living in the West, which I found so abhorrent. What I discovered in India was the condition of living in the "here and now," which didn't really make any difference how wealthy I was or what comfort there was. In the tea shop in India (where I lived for six months), I used to sleep on a wooden board. In the morning, three or four o'clock in the morning, as it began to get light, flies would crawl all over my bare back and tickle me awake. I was living the dream – not from the outside, of course – but inside, I was living here and now and was alive. I had no thought for the future, no ambitions for more, just appreciating the now moment.

And then I decided, "Oh, all very well; fun and all that, but time to get on with my life," so I came back to Europe. In Europe, they started it again: "What are you going to do? What are you going to become? I'm doing this. I'm doing that." I went to the mountains in North Scotland and threw the I Ching, hoping that it would say go to Africa or go to South America (because I didn't really fancy what I was seeing around me), and it said, categorically: "It benefits not a wise man to cross the water at this time. One should gain wisdom by overcoming adversity." Living on an island, there's not very far you can go without crossing water. So no Africa, no Far East, no America – none but Britain. I was a bit upset about it but it didn't make me think, "Okay, try again. Throw something else." It had told me what it had to tell and I had to deal with that.

I came back to London and I stumbled across an advert in a national daily paper, which described a job offer inviting people for a residential social work unit that they were just starting. They wanted people with relevant experience (but not specifically academic qualifications) to deal with 15 to 18 year-old emotionally disturbed, delinquent boys. So for two years I struggled, I got involved, I even got promotion at one point. I worked with these kids who really were the pits of the pit. It was what they call a secure unit with unbreakable glass, locked doors everywhere – almost a boys' prison, but they were too young to be prisoners. My special kid, he had 250 offenses against him by the age of 14: burglaries, car thefts, various things he had done. It was exhausting, emotionally draining for all of us. We had events which were so shocking that I couldn't conceive them. [There was] the kid who was so upset with life he took superglue and glued his eyes shut (he'd seen enough of the world, he told us later). Some dug the silicone out of the windows and shimmied down the drainpipes and ran away with nothing in their pockets. [I saw] things that seemed to be acts of desperation.

After a couple of years of that, I decided I'd done my bit and I accompanied a friend of mine who was moving to North Scotland. There I did the living off the land, the country, the hippy thing a little bit – not entirely irresponsible, part of a community but self-sufficient – living off my wits, we could say. All this time I had no goal for spiritual awakening but I had a definite goal for an emotional and an intellectual freedom. I was not prepared to accept the domination of the mentality and ideas which society was throwing at me.

I left Scotland, came to London and got some money together with the wild idea that I had to do something different. I flew to New York, hitchhiked to Mexico, went down to Guatemala – and I got this outrageous eye infection when I was in Belize on my way back. In Mexico, I was put in hospital and I had, through the next couple of days, an experience where I came finally to realize that the soul is a real thing; it exists. The body is the body but, within the body, the soul exists, and is the real me. I was put in conditions of pain and presence that made me realize: a) the stupidity of this running around thing, but also b) what we call in Sahaj Marg "the real goal of human life."

The point of my life was not what I had been doing all those years. I had been running around seeking pleasure and fun, all very anti-establishment. All these things gave way to an idea – forget the outside. Inside there is something far more beautiful, far more complete. Up to that point, I had ignored it. So then I realized I needed to find a technique, a way to unravel the mesh of my present consciousness and feel – realize the truth that what I had perceived in the isolation ward of the hospital was the real me. I was 29.

So I had a summer after that (by then 1980) of again resurrecting my economy and working. I met old traveling friends who had started Sahaj Marg in the early 1970's. They introduced me to a preceptor, a longhair rebel like me. I felt a brotherliness with him. He'd done the hitchhiking to India thing a few years before me and, by the time I met him, he was running a business renting out music equipment to young up-and-coming bands, all part of the underground music scene, which was where I came from too.

I went to see him on my own one afternoon and we spent a few hours and a few coffees talking about everything and he said, as I'm leaving, "But didn't you want a sitting?" "Well yeah…" "OK let's do it. Come." So he gave me my first sitting in this system. I felt nothing but said thanks. A month or so later, I decided, "Yes I'm going to go to India; I'm going to find a system of meditation or training that will help me realize this story again, the inner me. But, if I don't find it in India I will carry on." I would go to South America or go wherever but I thought the starting point should be India. Because I was going to India, I went back to see this guy John again. We spent another few hours and another few coffees talking about drugs and rock 'n roll and again he did the same thing as I'm leaving, "Oh, don't you want a sitting?" "Well, yeah, if you have time." [So he] gave me a second sitting. And then he said these wonderful words, he said: "Look if you're going to India, why don't you go and meet this Babuji? He probably has somewhere you can stay for a few days. Try it out. Maybe this would be the thing for you. You've got nothing to lose."

So I went to India and went back to my friend's farm in Punjab, left some things and said, "I'm just going off to find a guru (laughs). I don't know where I'm going to find him but maybe see you sometime." and I set off on foot to try and find a guru and a system of meditation. I was right up against the Pakistan border. North was mountains. South was desert. So east was the only way to go.

 I set off, stopping every now and again, but after about two weeks of this search I decided, "OK, this isn't going very fast and anyway, maybe I should go and see this one guy. At least I have this one's address; it's a start." The other well-known gurus were far, far away.

In Shahjahanpur, after running around, I found the ashram and went inside. They gave me tea and then later they said, "You can stay for dinner but you can't stay to sleep. You're not an abhyasi." "OK," I said but in my mind I thought, "Okay, well then if that's it, then I'll go. And that's the end." But then the caretaker says, "Look, you're not an abhyasi. You can't stay, but tomorrow morning you go to see Babuji. If he permits then you can come back. If he says yes, then you can come back."

In India, of course, in a small town there are no hotels so I went to the rail station and, at the rail station, I met a rather well-known abhyasi who was waiting to leave, catching his train. He was a Parisian fashion photographer, had photographed Babuji thousands of times, and was just waiting for his train. So I sat with him for an hour, two, three hours that night, talking about the practice, talking about Babuji, the system, a bit of Mission history, everything – and he told me, "Rickshaw. Take a rickshaw and pay not more than three rupees, and you're there."

So in the morning I got the rickshaw to Babuji's house. After a certain distance, the driver says, "Sorry, seven rupees." I said, "No, no, no. I was told three rupees. We agreed three rupees." Well, he disagreed, so I paid him off and stepped down from the rickshaw. Then I realized I didn't actually know Babuji's address. So I'm in the middle of Shahjahanpur with no address. I go to the nearest teashop and say, "Excuse me. Do you know where Babuji, Shri Ram Chandra lives?" and he says, "No. Never heard of him."(All in my best Hindi. It was all working quite ok, no misunderstandings.) At that moment in time, I could almost have just vanished.

Ten meters away there was a big concrete signboard, [indicating] Ram Chandra Mission and a finger pointing down a little, little lane you never would have noticed. If I had left the rickshaw half a kilometer away, no chance. I was right next to that signboard and the teashop right next to it had never heard about Babuji (laughs). I walked down this little street. There were ten houses or so on it and, after a number of houses, I came to feel that I'd certainly passed it. I turned around, examining each one as much by my feeling as by my vision. I came to one door which has a name on it – actually, the name of Babuji's father – but no "Shri Ram Chandra Mission," no "Babuji" but I could feel the bang, bang, bang in my heart saying, this is the place.

I walked in and the secretary hobbled across the floor (he had a leg problem) and said, "Come, come. You've come to see Babuji. Come, come. Sit." I recognized the man from the photo sitting in a chair [nearby] with his legs all wrapped up and no one around. He was sitting "taking the sun," as they call it. I get busy greeting him and so on and he says, "So, how are you?" and I say, "Fine" by reflex. He gestured for me to sit, which of course I did. And then, silence. For about half an hour, I sat there with him. Initially, I'm kind of expecting him to say something and processing all the different ideas I have because I have, in some way, to ask permission to stay at the ashram, ask what this practice is, what goal he's offering, all sorts of things are there, how to formulate these ideas. In the meantime, he just gazes at me, like a child almost, with blurry eyes, you know, he just gazes. I'm so self-conscious I think maybe he's looking for someone behind me but no, he's not. I gaze at him and I don't see him, I look through him almost. We locked our eyes together for some minutes and then a thought comes in my head (because the thoughts had stopped – what to ask, all that had stopped): "If I am as transparent to him as I feel I am, then he can see my questions. Therefore I don't have to ask." So, with that, I kind of relaxed. I felt naked in front of him and yet was so relaxed I sat back, with legs apart, in a posture of unnatural self-assuredness. I felt completely naked but still had the confidence not to erect defenses. Instead, I let him see through me, let him see what he wants to see. I had nothing to hide, nothing to project, so I just allowed him to gaze through me and make of it what he could.

After some minutes of silent gazing, he took out his hookah. It dawned on me even then that, if there's anything in this world I was good at, knew a lot about, it was smoking. I could smoke. I could roll cigarettes on the back of a motorbike. I had even made water pipes in the old days and sold them at festivals, you know? Smoking was my forte. And he sat there, smoked his hookah – without smoking. It was stunning; I was mesmerized.

The only comparable experience I've had was, some years later in Tunisia, watching some Bedouin pipers. A flautist was doing what they call circular breathing. He just played and played and played and played and played and didn't take a single breath. At the time, I was playing the flute in a folk music band in Denmark [so] I was really mesmerized by that.

I was mesmerized by Babuji's smoking, without smoking. He would put the mouthpiece to his lips, he would kind of inhale and he would blow out smoke but he didn't <u>do</u> anything. After a while, he just gave it back; it was over. But he just <u>showed</u> me non-doing doing. Staggering. He smoked without the DO-ing of it. Years ago in the mountain of Himalaya I remember being mesmerized, or amused anyway, by a little nine or ten-year-old kid scampering up and down the mountainside, collecting water from the river and every few minutes that shopkeeper would give him a moment off and he would take a little beedy and he would smoke it (inhales noisily, exhales forcibly). Babuji didn't do any of that. He put the thing to his lips, he inhaled, he took the pipe away, the smoke just came out of him, and then nothing, and then he did it again. He wasn't doing it – but he was doing it.

After that, a little guy came along, came up from behind him, and whispered into his ear. I later found out it was a doctor wanting to do a neck examination of Babuji, who apparently had some neck problem. So the doctor explained to Babuji and then he put his hands around Babuji's head and started twisting him. I thought this was altogether bizarre and totally disrespectful but anyway, if you've got to do it you've got to do it – and he did it. Babuji was blankness, total boredom, total disinterest. It was as though he was not even there – until a certain point was reached where the pain hit, you know, and then his face was transformed into that of a drowning baby, a drowning child, "Aaaaaaaa!" As soon as he moved away again, blankness. Then he did it the other side, "Aaaaa!" He did this four times. Each time Babuji went from absolute disinterest to absolute panic. It was very weird.

I'm kind of processing this when the secretary, the guy with the limp, comes up and taps me on the shoulder: "Babuji said you may go to the ashram now. You are permitted to stay for three days. You may start the practice. You are welcome to stay for three days." I looked at him. I look at Babuji. They hadn't been <u>near</u> each other let alone talk to each other (laughs). With a kind of innocence, I say, "Well, thank you Babuji" and I went to the ashram and started the practice. I had two sittings from a foreign preceptor who was there at the time. The third one, they said you can join the group satsangh now. So, on the second day itself I joined in the group satsangh with Babuji.

Different to that feeling with John in London, in the sitting with Babuji I could feel what I call a "flicker" in the heart. I could feel it start; I could feel it stop. It was delicate; it was gentle. It was light but it was tangible; it was palpable. In one of the group sittings he gave, I felt it stop. "Aw, ok, it's over." It was only a few minutes into the sitting but it stopped – so I opened my eyes, looked around – everyone else was meditating and he seemed to be in meditation too, so "Oh, ok" and I closed my eyes and sure enough, after a few minutes, it started again.

I felt I knew already, right at the beginning, that there was something in this. There was this otherworldliness about Babuji, which wasn't in any way how one would expect or anticipate, but it was there. I'd been in India some years already by then: I'd seen old Indians. I wasn't enamored or charmed by seeing a little old man sitting on the floor, you know? He had something different. It wasn't really that obvious but there was a feeling, when I was sitting in his house that first time, that my search was over, that I didn't have to carry on traipsing all over the world (that was done). And there was a feeling of being at home with him that was more "unthreatening," shall we say, than any home I'd ever been in – and I'm talking my own home and the place I'd had in the mountains. There was a sense of support and warmth and welcome that I hadn't felt elsewhere.

So, after three days, I'd taken my sittings, I'd joined in, and I was to go now. When I got to the gate after three days and wondered what to do, I thought, "Well, let's go and see Sister Kasturi. Two Danes had just come back from visiting her in Lucknow, and they had spoken superlatively about her. "Why not? It's only 175 kilometers down the road." So, after some adventures, I got to Lucknow and I met this Sister Kasturi. She was very different, or, at least, I felt the atmosphere was very different.

I'd heard a few words about her. She was the only senior female figure in the Mission at that time (that was talked about). She had known Babuji for 30 years or more, from when she was relatively young. She was Indian but not a healthy woman, so she never married. She lived with her brother. She was a devotee of Babuji like you talk of Krishna and Vivekananda. She was a senior devotee of Babuji, a *bhakta* of Babuji and almost a senior sister to Chari. If you read Chariji's autobiography and so on, he would always refer his dreams and his experiences to her to be referenced. She was the queen, the princess, whatever. She lived with her brother in the railway compound of Lucknow. She was maybe 50 by then, definitely older than myself, a mature lady.

I arrived. I introduced myself [to the brother]. "Oh, you've come to see my sister then. Ok, sit there." and he called Sister Kasturi to come. We chitchatted a while and then there was silence. After what was probably only a minute or two but it felt like a long time she looked up at me, looked straight at my heart and said, "And how is my Master?" It was like a shotgun straight in the chest. I was impaled by it. There was a strong powerful conviction, in fact – it was a feeling but it was a conviction too – this woman has only Master in her heart and in her sight. It was a force like nothing I'd ever experienced before [mimics lips flapping, heart pounding on chest]. I told her about how he came to satsanghs and so on and she was happy with that. Having said all these things, she said, "Okay, let's have the satsangh." and she called her brother and her sister forward and there was a small group of us and we had a group satsangh. My chest is banging like this [mimics pounding heart, panting] and there was no <u>question</u> of thinking. The physical reality of the heart was so strong that knee joints and thoughts vanished; it was all heart.

Then, after the satsangh was over, she says, "Well, if there's any question you have you can put it now." I said simply, "Look, I've just started this practice. I really feel I have to go away and practice. If I can, I'll come back and ask some questions in the future but just now (laughs)... There was some talk about where I was going to stay for the night but she said, "No, no, he's not staying." so without any indecision I left. It was clear. I was a greenhorn, you know? I went back to the station, I sat down, and I thought, "Well, look. I've started an Indian practice. I've got an Indian master. I've got nothing else in my life going on at the moment. I've got some friends in Punjab. Well, I'll stay in India! What the hell?"

Babuji then was age 81. It was 1980 and, at that time, we British didn't need an Indian visa. As a British citizen, I could live in India for the rest of my life; I just needed a valid passport. So I went back to Punjab and said, "Hi. I've decided to stay in India." My friends there said, "Well, great! Farm with us. Live with us. Be with us! You're one of the family." So I stayed there two and a half years. I lived on their farm. I farmed. Towards the end, I actually rented their cousin's farm, bought a tractor, and I farmed. Every few months I would go and see Babuji for a couple of days. At that time, Indians could only stay in the ashram for three days at a time. Babuji had said somewhere that he could do everything in three sittings. "Anyone who comes to me, in three sittings, I can give them everything that they can absorb, or consume or receive at that time, so there's no need for them to stay longer."

In 1982, he made this last trip to Europe. In 1980, Babuji had visited Europe and, due to health concerns, everyone thought that would be his last trip to Europe. But then he said his Master, Lalaji, had commanded that he go to Europe, so he came to Europe and we had a seminar in Paris. My money was running low in the Punjab and I came back to Europe with the idea of attending the seminar and also earning a little bit of money before going back to continue farming.

As soon as I came back to India in April of 1983, he (Babuji) had been in hospital for six months. I went to see him and he was at the end of his life. He was maybe 35 kilos. He was crumpled up on a gurney and had a tube in his nose but he was breathing naturally – like the smoking, breathing without breathing. You could see the ripple in his chest cage; that was the only signal that he was alive – that, and the sublime atmosphere radiating there, which was just the same as at the Shahjahanpur house. The transmission in the air was so tangible you could practically have felt it from the center of the city. It was wonderful! You look at him and you think, "How can it be? He looks so sick." and then you feel in your heart and you feel the expansion and love and all these things.

I had some work in Punjab so I stayed a few days and then went back to sort out some things and then I came back to Delhi two weeks later – and he was gone. He had died, been taken back to Shahjahanpur and cremated already. With that, I had the trauma, if you like, of: a) being told rather abruptly what had happened, but also b) the realization that the whole reason for my being in India was him, meaning it was gone. The practice, I knew already from my trip to Europe, I could do anywhere. There were preceptors throughout Europe. I didn't need to be in India except for him, but he was no longer there.

So the idea formed and by the end of the year, I'd moved to Europe, living in Denmark. I settled there, married there, and continued the practice there. The goal was still the same; the practice was the same - meditation, cleaning, and prayer - and an aspiration for a condition which was beyond all this materialism. During that time, Master [Chariji] had come to my house in Denmark and decided to make me a preceptor. We'd had a number of seminars, we'd bought the ashram in Augerans, I'd been to South France to seminars with him and we'd had a number of exchanges.

The problems I faced during those years stemmed from my kind of immaturity and my weakness in terms of emotional attachment and attraction and all these things. My stay in Denmark was eight years and, at the end of it, I was divorced. When the divorce happened, I went into a kind of meltdown situation emotionally and went off with a woman to France. When that didn't work out, I finally crawled back to England with my tail between my legs, and looked at these two letters Master had sent me, almost identical, saying, "Martin, I think you should return to your home. I believe you've been wasting your time, seeking security outside your own home" (outside Britain was how I understood it); trying to pin your security onto a wife, on a woman, on a country, on a profession, on a lifestyle – but it's not your own security.

The first time I couldn't hear it. The first time I didn't want England. I was having problems with the Denmark thing but the last thing I wanted to do was return to Britain. After the year in France, it was too obvious that he was right and I was wrong, so I returned to England and started making the changes in my emotional life and in my practical life that the practice demanded. Obviously, by then, drugs and all these things had fallen away but there were some things that really needed work. The main one, which I mentioned in my book and which I learned in that return to England, was humility.

I'd been play-acting the little farmer boy from India and probably accused of being arrogant or being childish and all these things. Humility was the main first lesson I had to deal with. I got a job in a Council Office. I lived with my mother. I wore a shirt and tie. I walked or drove to work, almost the same journey I made when I was 18. I was a data clerk in the local council, a million miles from farming in India (chuckles ruefully). I joined in. I did what I felt I could. We had satsangh in an old hall in London. I got involved with resurrecting the old British magazine The Natural Way and I was just living day-by-day doing what was right, you know, not focusing on the greyness of where I was living at that time.

In 1995, I came to Chennai and, by then, I was very much involved in the audio archives of the mission. As soon as I presented myself, I was given the keys to the computer room and told how/where to do the audio publications and was put in charge of the audio file archives and got really busy. The next year I came, I came on an open ticket and I said to Master, "Look, I can live in England if you want but I feel more useful here." and he said, "Yes, you're welcome. Please come." So he gave me permission to move to India. What I did then was present my first business plan (to manage apartments for various abhyasis, including letting apartments for short-stay visitors). I also started a taxi business and now I make eyeglasses.

Kim: What was going on with your spiritual evolution in the meantime?

I think there is an important element we skipped across and that is the Bhagavad Gita. The Gita is half a chapter in a bigger book called the Mahabharata. It's an old epic based on verbal tradition which was written down two and a half thousand years ago. In the middle of that is a little chapter. Krishna is there as an advisor – as a spiritual avatar but also as an advisor to a family that's in a battle situation. Arjuna doesn't want to fight. He goes into the middle of the battlefield. Krishna is his charioteer and Arjuna says, "How can I fight? On this side are my teachers, my cousins. On this side are my brothers and my other teachers. How can I kill them? How can I get any benefit from doing this?"

The Gita is the dialogue between these two on the battlefield. It's basically a description of karma yoga, karma yoga being the yoga of action as [compared to] the yoga of devotion, the bhakti (which I talked about with Sister Kasturi), or the jnana yoga, which is more the meditation or "study" yoga, if you like. Raja yoga, which is what we call our practice, is the yoga of meditation, the 'king' of yogas.

Karma yoga is the yoga of the body, of works – and this is what you will see a lot of in the ashram. There are people who don't seem to meditate a great deal, don't seem to take an awful lot of sittings, and don't seem to queue up at Master's door all that often. Their devotion to Master is through their action, not because they're trying to achieve anything. The three basic precepts of karma yoga are: i) one works without seeking the fruits of one's labor, ii) one works without feeling or believing one is the actor or do-er of that labor, and iii) one does everything merged in the consciousness of the divine.

In my book, I talk of the eighteenth birthday in the West. It used to be the twenty-first but now it's the eighteenth, when you become a man, maturity. In my culture, it was very common to have a big birthday party and lots of presents and all these things. I was a rebel by then already so I said I don't want a party, etc. but I do want the Bhagavad Gita. This was my only request; and my parents found a copy of the Bhagavad Gita. It's still there (points to it across the room); I still have it, forty years later. This was my sign of rebellion; but also, I'd heard about it, I'd read a little bit of it, I knew in some way what it was about.

They gave me this copy of the Bhagavad Gita and I've read it, on and off, over these years, and really it harmonized for me something I felt all that time. Doing for the benefit of doing was what I saw out in the West. BMW's [cars], flats [apartments], position in party, in politics, whatever – everyone was doing for gain. Here, karma yoga gave me, in a sense, a way to be and to live and to do – to be in the world, to act in the world – without mirroring that kind of obesity, grossness, whatever you call it.

It was through karma yoga and through the <u>Bhagavad Gita</u> that I became interested in an alternative way, a spiritual way. It was through that story in the hospital that I was spring-boarded into realizing that the soul existed and that the divine was within, not without. It was through the practice of Sahaj Marg and the meditation that I realized that it was like a flower unfolding. I didn't have to <u>do</u> anything. You know, when you're farming you have to water but the growing it does itself. This is what I felt was happening for me, that Sahaj Marg was feeding that flowering within and I didn't have to <u>do</u> anything on that level. I didn't really have to do the other stuff too but, you're here, you're involved, you want to be useful. That was really a key element of my request in the beginning to Master, when I wanted to move here; I could be more useful here. So my target has been during these years to be useful, not just to abhyasis but also to the world.

In these 30 years of practice, I've had a number of experiences, shall we say, or glimpses of something beyond – but that is no longer the purpose of doing the practice. I'm not after experiences; I'm not after ringing bells or whatever you like to call it. We are on a road, on a journey of Sahaj Marg. We're on a path – and it's the right path for me, so I'm on it to the end of the road, almost wherever that road takes me. There are times I'm a bit less than perfect, times I'm a little lazy, a little diverted here and there but really, I barely question the validity of it anymore. The vital, the real essence of the journey was the beginning. It's like the archer, you know? You see the target. You focus. But once the arrow is gone, then you've got to let it fly to the target. In the old, old, old, old days, I remember people talking about certain experiences they liked or disliked or wanted. I've heard preceptors say, "Oh, after you start Sahaj Marg, you will feel this and you will feel that, and all these problems will go away." That is not what it is about. It's about something far deeper than that. And if that grip of comprehension and conviction is strong enough, then the passing experiences are secondary. So I don't really have a whole list of graduated experiences to recall or to record.

Kim: What advice would you have for people who are just starting, maybe, to think about spirituality?

I was a preceptor for 16 years. My experience has always been that the Westerners need to know "why" to meditate. The Indians only seem to care about "how" to meditate. And the "why" is a personal thing. I would try to imagine someone going back to being 18 or 20 or 30 and looking around and not finding any real sense of it all. They have to look inside because outside, they'll find (we all find) attraction and diversion. If we are just on this planet to party, eat, have fun and then die – if that is the reason – then doing an austere practice would be a waste of time. My experience is that many people I've met in Sahaj Marg have in fact had strife in their life, be it divorce, be it lost family members, be it hardship in childhood, be it even more grotesque histories. However, all of these things, in some way, have forced the person to ask, "What is life all about? What is to be had from living?" I guess that time of life comes differently to different people.

This, Sahaj Marg, for me, is my way but it's not the only way, I'm sure of it. If it works for me, for you, for someone else, then it's great! If they need something else [then] open your eyes. Look. It should be obvious. To us all who've started to feel inside, it is obvious. The world is in meltdown, chaos. Material aspiration might secure a degree of supposed security and comfort but only for a length of time. Sooner or later, you're going to have a colostomy bag on your belly, you're going to have a walking stick, and you're going to have miseries to hang onto. The life of the body is limited in many ways. The life of the material world, of wealth, is limited in material ways – not to mention all this envy and jealousy and all the other things. There's so much ugliness in the world that we can become immune to it. We can accept it, understand it, and deal with it in ways that don't bring us down. And that is miserable in a sense, that more people don't realize that and start working at finding ways – not to become immune – but simply to be able to deal with the realities that daily life throws up.

Kim: Do you see Sahaj Marg as a pathway or sign of hope, a social movement to help us deal with the future?

I would say yes and no – but yes, definitely. There are an extreme number of material obstacles to the survival of the species at the moment. I'll start by giving a fun story about that because, years ago, Chari said something similar. "We should prepare for the end of the world," was what he said. The preceptor in charge of Denmark came back from India: "Chari has said we should…" (trumpeting voice). You would not <u>believe</u> what they got up to. People were buying sacks of wheat and sticking them away, and bunches of batteries and thermal underwear; you wouldn't believe what people were doing. "The end of the world is coming!" It was fun, because my preceptor at the time was a saxophonist. He was a jazz saxophonist and I said, "Well, what are you gonna do?" and he said, "Well, what can I do? I'm a saxophonist." (laughter) "I will play. I will write my music. I will play – you know, like the violinist on the <u>Titanic</u> [sinking ship] or something. Do what you can but don't lose yourself in all this emotional blah blah blah." That was his take on it and, a week or two or three later, we got this letter from Master to everyone in the world, "So and so has got it wrong. I did not say this. Please stop this behavior." Stop behaving like loonies, you know.

But yes, a saxophonist can only play his music, live a good family life, and be as kind as he can to his neighbors and (the concept that I use in my book), willful restraint. We realize that the population is too great. What are we doing creating two babies, three babies, four, five babies per family? What are we doing using gas-guzzling cars to go down to get a newspaper? We can take a bicycle. There are very simple adjustments that we can make on a very human local level which are wise to do. Whether you are an abhyasi or not is not the issue. I personally don't want to wind all this up in Sahaj Marg because, what you're talking about is humanity, which is the whole group. Don't join Sahaj Marg to change the world. Join Sahaj Marg to change yourself. You changing will change the world – and whether you've done it through Sahaj Marg or through some Sufi mystic, it doesn't matter. If it changes the world for the good, then good. If it doesn't, it's not so good.

I take Master as an inspiration, if you like, but also as a guide. He talks with great joy about The Foundation series of books by Asimov (1951). This is special. Eighteen thousand years down the road humanity has, in a sense, populated the universe. There have been no mutations and all these funny things, no super telepathy, etc. But certain scientific breakthroughs have come, which we would fully expect to come because our brains are deductive and smart.

There's something within humanity which we don't see in the animal kingdom – and the simplest way to call it is first "mind" but also "love." This quality of humanity, I feel, could be (most wondrously) distributed throughout the galaxy, the universe – IF we could get through the next few generations, decades, or centuries even, of human mess. If we can do that, then there's a possibility for humanity to create a kind of longevity within itself – not to become more powerful, but simply to spread that love, the nobility of humankind throughout the universe.

The Majesty, the nobility of humanity could go beyond our solar system; and that, I look upon, as being a kind of global goal of life. The individual goal of life is merging in the oneness of the Divine. I see him (Chari) as having done [this mergence] already, and Babuji before him – and this is a potential for an individual human. That is my goal – but, there could be a collective goal of humanity which is well, well, <u>well</u> beyond simply surviving another generation, and another generation.

Actually, there are forums in place, for example: Oxford University's Future of Humanity Institute and the Cambridge Centre for the Study of Existential Risk (see references and resources) have already taken this up. They are studying the real threat humanity poses against the whole of humankind – and solutions outside the solar system are only one part of the remit. But I think we each have to look upon our individual goal of life and the possibility of attaining a condition within ourselves which is as close to Divine as possible. This higher condition will have a benefit on the immediate environment (our family, our children, our neighbors, our village, our community) and can also influence our professional responsibilities, with the possibility of taking humanity onwards. This lies intrinsically in what I am doing with my book, as a way of getting that message out.

Doomsday is, of course, always there. I Googled it not long ago. Ninety percent of all species known to humans are now extinct. Ninety percent – that's a very large number. Not just a dodo, a mammoth, this or that and one or two. Ninety percent of all the fossilized species that they've catalogued and recorded are now extinct. And there are more every year, so what chance humanity? We have to have a bigger vision besides survival, [besides] grabbing and stealing from nature. We have to get beyond that and we have to realize our humanity. Sahaj Marg supplements that, it is good for that. <u>But the sole purpose is the spiritual evolution of the individual.</u> I don't meditate for anyone else. I meditate for me but the effect of that meditation is there for everyone else – so I'm happy, they are my brothers, my sisters and, if I can be of use to them, I will. But I can't change them, not directly.

Something we haven't really talked about, which I think is vital in all of this, and in the life of every abhyasi too, is the need to change our relationship with the mind. Mind energy is what has created the mess we're in. Mind energy is what is pushing people to the limits of what they're doing now – "Non-Think" is what I call it – and a change in the mind will naturally change the path of humanity. We do have to change the way we think. You know, an obvious example – violent movies make a child have bad dreams. A negative thought has a negative effect, albeit very small. Cumulatively, there are a thousand million people in India and, if all those thousand million people are angry about something, you can believe it; you will see pockets of behavior which are totally outrageous. You pick up any Indian newspaper and you'll see, "so and so hacked to death." Because of what? Fights, behaviors, bizarre events in the world – a lot of it is to do with uncontrolled, negatively-forged mental activity.

There was a train driver in Spain recently, who posted on Facebook or something messages like, "See how fast I'm going! If I was driving a car, I'd be done for speeding." He was driving one of these superfast trains and he got away from himself, drove 190 through an 80 kilometer speed limit, went round a corner, the whole train went over and more than 80 people are dead now because of this uncontrolled egoistic act, a mind flip of, "See, I am in charge." This is what humanity has done.

I Googled recently how many people have died through the act of dictators in the twentieth century and there were hundreds of millions of people! Pol Pot in Cambodia, this one in this place, that one in that place, Hitler of course – people with outrageous aspirations and delusions of grandeur or power, of correctness or rightness – have created absolute mayhem. All those people who died had potential for taking humanity onwards rather than just vanishing.

When I started my job as a social worker, in my interview, I clearly remember being asked what my faith was, what my beliefs were. I said, "Well, my belief is in the human being overcoming adversity." I had a belief in humankind over and above the obstacles that we have placed before us. Now it is somewhat the same, but I cannot rely on them. I cannot rely on someone else to solve our problems, my problems. If we give in to this laissez-faire attitude that it doesn't matter, then we have to take the consequences. I believe firmly that the population of the world is already more than 50% of what it needs to be or should be. In another 50 to 60 years, it could be double what it is now. What will we eat? Where will we all live? So we have to make some serious advances technologically, scientifically – but in parallel, we have to make some serious advances emotionally and mentally. The spiritual organizations (and Sahaj Marg is purely that) have an enormous relevance to it all. So we're talking about a different dimension but a vital dimension to the survival of the species.

Kim: To close, can you tell us more about your book?

That's sweet of you. It started a while back when I was on retreat in the Himalayas. I was looking out over the plains of North India at dusk and I just felt the need to paint my particular canvas of words, to describe the vision of life that I had built up over the years. I started a while later, penning down some of the events of my life, and the book grew out of that. Now, due to the volume of material, it has been trimmed down to tell the unfolding adventures of my life in relation to the growth of clarity in what we could call seeking my personal goal in life. The title says it all: To be all a man can be: The journey of a lifetime (Worthy, M.).

We've covered much of it in the interview, but I have really tried to reveal the gestation of ideas and attitudes as I evolved out of that postwar, hippy era, how I avoided all the side traps and kept on keeping on seeking an inner goal, a condition. Babuji said it once in his discreet way, "You want riches, what for? So you can buy an airplane? But I am in an airplane, flying, is it not the same?" What possessions give you are headaches; the Sadhus of India will tell you the same. What I have been seeking all this while is inner happiness and equanimity, the joyful state of wonder and appreciation that lie at the end of this rainbow life I have been living, *sahaj samadhi* (see glossary).

So, my last chapter is my attempt at describing the goal, the height of man's potential, the inner condition that is beyond whether we have a new car or ride a bicycle – the inner state that puts the material struggle in perspective for what it is: scrabbling in the dirt. I scrabble around too, I work, I do my best, I try to let go of egoistic attractions and be useful to others, but not just for weighing up at the end of the day how much dirt I collected!

The book? Hopefully in print by mid-2015.

Chapter 10

Belief, Trust, Faith, Love

Mumbai Newlyweds: 2 brothers & their wives

late 20's/ early 30's, media broadcasting & technology/ engineering

Brother 1, Brother 2
Sister 1, Sister 2 (sisters by marriage)

Preface: I hurry out the back door of the ashram, worried I might miss the family who has agreed to be interviewed. I thought we were meeting at the canteen, but they had already gone to the garden at my friend's house nearby. They were already nervous about giving the interview, asking several times to make sure we had approval for the project, and I didn't want them to change their minds. I thought there would be five of them (two newly married couples and the mother of the two sons) but, when I see them in the distance walking back my direction, it seems there will only be the two men. I am disappointed, but still happy the brothers have agreed to meet me. I know they are modern, hip, successful, and up-and-coming and am curious to hear their thoughts and insights about spirituality, especially when speaking to those still focused on materialism.

We settle in the garden and try to ignore construction noise nearby as we chat. Happily, their young wives join us a few minutes later. It is sometimes difficult to take turns and keep the recorder in front of the correct mouth!

In this somewhat rollicking chapter, join an animated discussion between Kim and these two couples who are modern yet traditional Indians. Discussion topics range from the difference between religion and spirituality to how one becomes a good parent.

Kim: Would you talk about your background? I'm guessing you're from India. I know your brother is here too.

Brother 1: We were born in a small town in India, into a Hindu family. I did my Engineering and then I did my PhD and moved into a job in Mumbai. He [my brother] also completed studies and moved into a job in Mumbai. He is in the media line and we have been in Mumbai now for the past eight years.

Kim: So you both live together? And are you both married?

Yes [we live together and] both of us are married. I got married about a year and a half ago and my brother was married about two months ago. Our wives are just arriving, in fact. (introductions)

Kim: Are you a typical family?

Brother 1: We are a typical family, but now we are more of a Sahaj Marg family. We were a traditional family. My father used to chant mantras and we would do all those Hindu rituals. Even when I was at school, I used to read the Hanuman Chalisa (see references) after bath. There is a festival known as Navratri and all nine days I used to read Durga Chalisa and I used to recite her chants. So we were a very traditional Hindu family, back then.

Now, everything has gone. No rituals, nothing. We are enjoying the way the Master tells us to meditate. This has become our life. When I look back at my [extended] family, they are still engrossed in all that. But we are not like that. If I tell people they may not understand, but I have to try.

Kim: How did you get involved with Sahaj Marg?

Brother 1: We were traveling back from Bangalore where I had exams – me, my brother and my mom. We were coming back on the train around July. It must have been in 1999 after Master's celebration, when people were returning to their homes. It was a long journey, about 48 hours. In the mornings, we saw them [other passengers] closing their eyes – this was on the train – and again in the evening, they used to close their eyes. In between, they were completely normal people like us. My mom became very inquisitive. They were normal people, but at a particular time, they would all close their eyes. What was this all about? Are they sleeping? But they cannot sleep all together. My mother asked one of the ladies what they were doing. They replied that they belong to a Mission with a guru and do meditation.

That was our first introduction to meditation. We were not feeling so interested. Only my mother was more serious; we just listened to our mom as she was having this conversation and they gave her a preceptor's details. My mother took the details and we all returned to our colleges. Then one day my mother remembered that we had met someone on the train and she had a phone number. She called and explained that she had been given the number on the train and wanted to know more about Sahaj Marg. So the preceptor invited my mom and dad and they went to the first sitting. My mom was more interested and my dad accompanied my mom. So that's how we got into this Sahaj Marg.

We were studying in college and had all the normal peer pressure and so many things coming up. My mother encouraged us [to do meditation] but we were all into the religious aspect, including my mom. About two years later, I told my mom that I also wanted to practice meditation. My brother and I were introduced to the preceptor, whose brother used to practice Reiki. He was with a Reiki master and I was interested in Reiki. So I ended up going to him, me and my brother both went to learn Reiki from him [the brother of the preceptor]. During our vacation time, my mom fixed an appointment with the preceptor and we started. My brother felt something, but I did not feel anything. I did not feel anything and, to this day, I have not felt much, but there is some kind of invisible rope that is connecting me to my Master. Other people have experiences and I have not. It's been about ten years.

Kim: Had you been looking for a guru?

Brother 1: No, in fact we didn't know about gurus. There were some saints in Hindu religion but I had never thought there had to be a guru. Maybe I was too young or not that mature.

Kim: Do you think it's important to have a religious background, to have a pure family lifestyle in order to come into Sahaj Marg?

Sister 2: Yes I do, because, when we take birth [after we are born], first we go to school and then we go for higher study. Religion is just a basic thing that teaches us how to keep ourselves disciplined, to obey our elders, and so on, in a disciplined manner. And then we have to go further. After religion, we have to move up to spirituality. So it's just like going from school to college, from college to master's degree and so on. Religion is needed for the basic upbringing.

Kim: That's really interesting, because I think you may have an advantage in India. It's not like in the States where people are going out and getting drunk and so on. I think there are more expectations of self-discipline (but maybe I'm over generalizing). Do you want to comment on that?

Brother 1: We don't have extremes.

Kim: As an outsider, I see you as clean-cut. I mean you are really hip, but still clean-cut.

Brother 1: It's not about clean. Master says that cleanliness is not something outside; it has to be inside. Maybe I, as an Indian, am not into wild extremes, but my thoughts could be. My actions might not be, but my thoughts could be. And that's equally dangerous. It might seem a small advantage but it might not be because, I may not be showing it, but it could be inside me. This is also negative because people from the West, they are showing it all. In India, we may have it there inside us but we cannot show it because of societal pressure and family values. But if it is there inside, this could be more dangerous.

Kim: Is there a conflict between religion and Sahaj Marg?

Brother 1. Yes, yes, yes. Even after getting introduced to Sahaj Marg, my family used to continue regular religious practice. It was like floating in two streams. We were doing meditation and doing religion, everything. For two or three years, I used to continue and there was always a question there in my mind: Should I leave religion, something I was born in, my parents and grandparents and everyone used to follow? There are so many Gods in Hindu mythology. How can I leave? It could be due to some kind of fear. I met with a senior preceptor once and I asked the same question, "How should we treat the Gods and Goddesses? What should be our feelings towards them?" Then she said "love." I did not understand anything. I said, "Okay, let me skip this" (laughs).

So it was a year or a year and half after that I read somewhere and heard Master talking about this point, that one should not leave religion, one should pass <u>through</u> religion. That one word caught my attention and every doubt was cleared. We need not leave religion; we have to pass <u>through</u> religion.

Kim: So, as I think Babuji said, spirituality begins where religion leaves off.

Brother 2: Exactly. I don't think we should demean the importance of religion. It is very important. It creates a base.

Without a base, you cannot have a foundation. We need to have a base. At least you know you have to trust someone. What do you learn in religion? You learn that you have to have faith in something unknown. In spirituality, if you don't start with faith, at least, at some point, you've got to have trust in something, so this is the point I am going to start with. Master says to trust the faith and everything develops from there.

Sister 2: You have to live in religion but it's very bad that we die in religion. You have to move further.

Kim: You know, I'm kind of jealous of all of you. Here you are, three couples (the parents, the two brothers and two sisters-by-marriage). Master made me cry this morning because I was just feeling alone, really lonely in my family, as I'm the only one who meditates.

Sister 2 answers: I was doing my meditation alone for seven or eight years and my family was into religion and not into this meditation. Once I got a chance to meet Master and I told him my parents are not in Sahaj Marg, that I was alone in Sahaj Marg and I faced many problems. He told me, "Don't worry. I'll take care of your parents." That day I left everything to him and now my parents are abhyasis. Just before my marriage, they asked me to kindly take them for the sittings and I took them for the sittings. It's all <u>his</u> wish.

Kim: So I need to go and see Master? It's hard to get in and see Master.

Sister 2: Inner Master. It's good to make contact with the inner Master. Surely, you will get some direction of where to go and how to go. Surely, you will get your answer.

Kim: Could you tell us a little bit about yourself?

Sister 1: I am a newsreader. Before marriage, I was reading news for a regional channel and then I got transferred into their Delhi head office. Then my marriage got fixed so I had to leave my job.

Kim: Why?

Because that was in my town. My husband and I are now in Mumbai. Now I'm trying to get a job in the media sector which will suit me.

Brother 1: Then our marriage got fixed.

Kim: When you say your marriage got fixed, can you explain?

Brother 1: Yes. Sure. I always wanted to marry a girl who is an abhyasi. By 2011, my father was still holding on to some family values and all. He wanted the girl to be from the same community and all. We are the only two sons. I surrendered myself and I accepted whatever Master's wishes were. We were married 26th or 27th November 2011. I'm sorry (laughs), the 26th. Around that time, we knew that Master was going to come to Banares, which is close to our hometown Patna. He was supposed to come a few days after our wedding, the 6th or 7th of December. So my mom thought it would be a good idea if all of us can go and meet Master.

Kim: So your marriage was kind of arranged by your parents?

Brother 1: Yes. Everything was arranged by family. We only sent the photos to Master and he approved it.

Kim: Did you know each other?

No.

Kim: Not at all?

Sister 1: When the marriage was fixed, we had some dates to try to get to know each other because we didn't know each other because our parents fixed our marriage. I had no objection.

Kim: But you were ready to get married?

Brother 1: Yeah. I thought, "Whatever our parents decide, I'll go for it."

Kim: I live in a Chinese culture where arranged marriage is fairly common. It's interesting for me to meet young, well-educated, "hip" people, as I was saying, yet you agree to an arranged marriage. From my cultural point of view, it is a little strange. The Chinese say the parents know better than the children.

Sister 1: Yes. Yes. I was always thinking that, whatever our parents think, I will go for it.

Kim: I wonder if you have any memories, stories, anything unusual to share with us (about your spiritual life)?

Brother 2: Stories of miracles should be avoided. So we have to purify our mind, thoughts and actions. We should come from fixed thinking to free thinking; let it be right, let it be wrong, let's go to open thinking. So when we talk of Eastern culture and Western culture and religion and spirituality, what exactly are we trying to prove? We want to prove that there is someone above us and that [someone] is a supreme power. Hindus, Catholics and everyone agrees that there is someone. It is good to be born in religion as we know we are not a superpower. A superpower is someone/something that is inside me, all around me, which is looking after each and every aspect of my life.

Then comes knowing spirituality is inside. I have to do a deep dive into myself to look for this secret gem. A lot of people come to Sahaj Marg when we have a little trouble in our life.

Very few have come for what we call "self-realization." We tend to come to spirituality when we are troubled at some point.

Sister 2: Life is very stressful, that's why. When there is depression, pressure and stress, they want to run away from all these things. They come here to be with themselves.

Brother 2: When we look very closely and examine ourselves, we have created all those webs. The moment we die, it's finished – nothing. You have created all those webs everywhere. Relationships are not heavy baggage; we should enjoy them. In life we are always trying to prove ourselves, what we are, what I am, she is good, he is good. We should enjoy [the present] like we are sitting here (gestures to group). Let us enjoy each other's company. The person next to you should enjoy your company.

So when we come here and start practicing, we don't really know what Master is. We see him in a body and see an 80-year old frail-bodied guy. What is Master and what can he do? Can he read my mind? Will he choose my destiny or do this or that? What can he do? But, slowly and gradually, once you start doing your practice, maybe not all your worries are over, but you will get a very relaxed feeling, very peaceful.

When we are inside a problem, we can never solve a problem. We have to be outside the problem so we can see the solution and solve the problem. Then your materialistic life will take a dramatic turn. Everything will take place in time. You don't know why, but you will start loving that guy, the Master, without thinking about yourself and what you get. You will just start loving him and you don't know why. You want to see him and you don't know why. Then you come to see what divinity is and then, after religion, this is when spirituality begins. After spirituality ends, reality begins. After reality ends, bliss begins. After bliss begins, oneness begins. This is the cycle of human evolution.

Kim: I'm going to be a skeptical Westerner. Two problems: 1) the idea of past lives and samskaras and 2) the idea of a living Master.

Brother 2: Very good questions and very true questions. Believing in past lives… but I will ask you a simple question. Why is it that some children are born very healthy in a happy family and another child has no hands or legs? Why would God distinguish this child? If you have a point, you should back it up. Just say why.

Kim: Religion didn't make sense to me and that's why I was so attracted to Sahaj Marg because it made sense. My minister (religious teacher) probably would have said that there was some kind of sin, or that one child was more loved by God. It doesn't make any sense to me.

Brother 2: God loves everyone in the same way. How could you differentiate between your children? Nothing matters. Open your heart. Accept others, love others, feel others.

Now we are coming to the second part. We finished the first part about reincarnation. God is always the same for everyone. He cannot make one child healthy and another with missing limbs. It's samskara. Do you know what samskara is? Samskaras are the effects of our actions as well as of our thoughts. In Hindu, it is Karma. Karma only talks about action – whatever I have done, that I will get. In samskaras, or impressions, it is also what I have thought. That means you become what you think you are.

Kim: Samskaras – anything that brings you great joy can also leave an impression, as well as something that brings you great sorrow. I have some trouble with that. I don't know if I want to lose those big joys. Even positive impressions you have to wash out, as well as the negatives.

Sister 2: Impressions live inside us whether positive or negative because they are alive inside the heart. For example, if you like something, if you like a rose and if you find it a beautiful flower, see it in constant remembrance of Master. What beauty Master has given this flower! [simply observing] If you love a rose flower and you go, "Wow, it's a beautiful flower," feeling it creates an impression. We don't want impressions, either good or bad. Master says that we have to become neutral – no good, no bad, blank. This means nothingness. Nothingness should be there. So whether good or bad, it's an impression. It can be good and give you tears and it can be bad and also give you tears. So good or bad, we don't want to keep impressions in ourselves. We keep away samskaras if we don't create impressions in ourselves. Thank you.

Brother 2: I'll give you an example. When you say you're confused about good and bad impressions, it's just like you have a balloon and it has to go high in the air and it is held by ten cases of chocolate or ten cases of garbage. If you have to float that balloon up in the air, what do you have to do? You have to cut both of them. It cannot float high in the air with either ten cases of chocolate or with ten cases of garbage. So you have to cut the bags of chocolate and you also have to cut the ten bags of garbage. It's the same with impressions. Here on earth when we have impressions, we cannot be raised to the next level. You can enjoy licking off the chocolate, but it will not float high.

Brother 2: Happiness is something which is always dependent. For example, "If my child will act like this, I will be happy." So happiness is always conditional, but joy is unconditional. You can never lose joy but you can lose happiness. So what is bliss? Bliss is unconditional joy. It is not a feeling, it is a state of being, a condition. That can never be lost by doing cleaning, by doing this and by doing that. You are becoming more and becoming larger in this condition. This is a natural kind of evolution. This is the answer.

Kim: He (your brother) says he can't feel during the meditation. What do you feel when you're meditating? Do you feel connected all the time? Do you feel bliss all the time?

Brother 2: I cannot say what I feel throughout the entire one hour of meditation, and it is probably what you feel. It's like knowing how to cook. Suppose you ask me what is an orange and I tell you it's a fruit with pulp and a sweet, tangy taste, etc. It wouldn't really make any sense to you. You have to taste it to know it, and possibly cultivate it, if a taste that is quite unusual in your home culture. This is known as sensitivity.

Kim: But you were talking about bliss as a state of being? Are you there?

Brother 2: How can a person say somebody is here and somebody is there? It is a state of unconditional love. Now we are having two levels of remembrance. One for our material world and secondly, for our divine world.

Now I will come to your last question – why this Master? Generally, people are not into this level. We are stuck in our material problems and we don't want to get into our divine problem. This speech of yours or your acts should benefit everyone. You are bounded by Kim. Kim is the name of a body, not of a soul. So your responsibilities should be to the whole world.

Now the last part. It has been said, "Why a living Master?" Many Westerners, especially our American friends, have a big problem accepting a person as a supreme [being]. He has never said that he is, never. We should accept him as someone who is more evolved. In your American culture it is always me, me, me; I have to build a house, I have to build a family, I have to buy a Ferrari. It's always about me. So what happens if these things go wrong? What happens if you have a toothache? Do you fix it yourself? You have to go to a doctor. Why? Because they can fix it. Similarly, some person who knows about divinity, you have to go to that person to know divinity, don't you? How will you manage, especially if you don't know anything about divinity, your [entire] lifetime? You go to your family, you read books and you have done this and that. By just reading medical books, can someone become a doctor?

Kim: I think of it as us being splintered off from the divine when we were created, however that happened with human beings. Like sparks, the creative force is spread throughout these sparks and basically what we're doing is trying to find our way home.

Brother 2: Yes. That is the language of an abhyasi.

Kim: So what do you think? Am I close? Is that right?

Brother 2: You are very close, dear. There's always what we think about God from our childhood. Everybody has a different idea about Him. Especially from childhood, like when you are angry with your parents, you declare that you don't believe in Him. We might say, "We don't believe in you, Krishna, Jesus" as an innocent reaction.

Now we come to spirituality; the word "spirituality" is made up of the Middle French *spiritualite*. That it is an evolutionary process for [becoming] sacred. Thinking about something continuously, this is meditation. And thinking about God continuously is?

Kim: Constant remembrance.

Brother 2: Yes. First you have to understand what our Mission says about humanity, how we are born. You said before about a spark, why was there a spark? Because energy power cannot be stagnant. Like water, stagnation will make it spoiled, or gross. So there was a spark and when there is a spark, that thing (shower) comes out. There may have been a God where it started and slowly it turned into minerals. That's the same thing, same divinity. Now somewhere between these minerals and God, we humans are here. Below that, there are animals like birds. Some said we have come from here (below) but I say, no, we have come from here (above).

Kim: So we have de-volved and we are trying to evolve back up.

Brother 2: The only thing is to evolve. I will tell you a very interesting thing. Not only do livings beings have life and death but every minute, every feeling. Suppose I tell you a joke and you laugh. That is the life of the joke. When you stop [laughing], it dies. So preserve the moment. Live it fully before it dies.

Brother 1: I was very short-tempered at one point in time. Suppose you told me something, it would haunt me; like, "OK, Xxx, you're bad." That used to haunt me for weeks. Not even days, for weeks! Why is someone calling me bad? Why did someone shout at me? Or if I had a fight with someone, that used to haunt me for so many days. Now, I don't care. If you say something to me, it's okay. It's like you're hitting on a damp surface and it's gone. There are no ripples. If you take that as an example of change, yes it is.

That's probably one of the reasons I'm in Sahaj Marg, because, while I don't see any apparent changes in me, I'm seeing those inner changes, which I myself have gone through. I may not experience things in meditation, but outside of it, I experience so many things, so many things. There's a gradual change that happens. I see myself ten years ago, five years ago, one year ago; and it is a change and I am sure it is going to continue. Looking back, there have been so many things that have been removed. It's a gradual journey and I know there are still things that have to be removed. This is what Sahaj Marg has helped me with. Whether you realize it or not, if you follow the system and you are sincere about the system, you get the benefit.

For a new person who may not be interested in spirituality, but who is interested in self-development, this is where they have to be. From self-development, they will find out where they can go next.

Kim: Master can help with spiritual development and character development.

Brother 1: Exactly. In fact, what Master says is that, if character is not developed, spirituality is immaterial. You need to have a developed character in order to progress in spirituality.

Brother 2: You will only accept those things which your heart has accepted; no superimposing. Like in our Eastern thing, if my mother said something to me, it is this and you have to do something like that. We may start doing that. The people of our generation will start doing that. But what is good about you guys is that you first analyze this. If that thing is good for you, you will do it. If you like it, you'll do it; otherwise, you will not do whatever it is. Now this is what makes you guys attracted to spirituality. Most people in the West feel that, even though they have everyone in their life, somehow we are all alone. There is no one to share the deepest secrets. We require one person to whom we can pour out anything, at any time and in any form.

So we all have done something. There is no need to carry the baggage. Come to the meditative world. It's not only Master but it's you who have to decide and make the effort.

Sister 1: Belief, trust, faith, and then love come.

Kim: So he wants my heart but not for him. He wants my heart for me, so that I can change. You are the only one who can change yourself. I understand.

Kim: Many people think our society, our Earth, is in a time of perhaps cataclysmic change. Can you comment on Sahaj Marg as a social movement?

Brother 2: It makes no difference if I say it is or it isn't a movement, or if some calamities will come. How does it make a difference? Why are we so worried about the future? No, we should look at the present. My universe ends with me. What happens after that, I am not there to see. I should be more concerned in this life about achieving what I have to, rather than waiting for the future or changing the entire world. How about today? Am I wasting my time or utilizing my time?

Kim: Is it important that you are a model for other people? Don't you think you have an obligation to help other people?

Brother 2: Yes, but I am responsible for myself first. If I am improved, my world around me will improve. If I progress, the world around me will progress. It makes no sense to be stagnant and ask others to move forward. People might listen to you for a few moments, but then they will rubbish [dismiss] you. First, you need to make some serious steps towards your own progress. Then, people will be attracted by you, will identify with you. Otherwise, it all becomes a philosophy. There are many philosophers who are in schools and colleges, but how many can be taken to the next level? So if you ask me, I need to improve and, if I improve, the world around me will improve. My universe ends with me.

Brother 2: This is a good line for your book. If you try to change the whole world, the whole world will change you. If you try to change yourself, you will change the whole world.

Kim: Thank you. I have one more question I was not intending to ask, but, you are all about at an age where you might be considering children. How has the practice of Sahaj Marg influenced your attitude toward parenting? Have you thought about that?

Brother 2: That's a very interesting question. To be a good parent, you need to be a good child. If you have parents, you need to be a good son or a good daughter. I think Sahaj Marg teaches you to be a good human being and, if you are a good human being, you'll automatically be a good son or daughter and eventually a good parent. If you are not a good son or daughter, you can never be a good parent. Until and unless you change as a person – and then everything changes. That's what I think. The past haunts if we stay the same but, if we change, then we are not the same person [and can move on]. I hope you understand. (smiles)

Brother 1: Master said you never have children. Children are always of God, so you are just a trustee.

(Listener): Khalil Gibran says that parents are the bow and children are the arrow. Therefore, if the bow is flexible enough and not too tight, if the bow is not too smooth, you are able to release it at that point, [and] the arrow goes straight to the goal. But if you restrain the arrow from being released, you drop it. I love that idea, parents being the bow and children being the arrow. (Everyone nods)

Brother 2: We are all small kids, even if our bodies are 60 or 70, so jump. Free your thinking, free it from yourself. Be totally free from all your thoughts, from all your anger, from all your attributes. Be free and enjoy life.

Brother 1: Have faith.

Brother 2: You have come with a purpose, not just for spirituality. Nothing is by chance. The only thing is our own mental blockages and our willingness. Am I really willing to accept what I have heard, what we have said here? One person in your life is sufficient to change your life, even if you read many inspiring books.

Sister 2: We are lucky to have such a good Master.

Brother 2: Let your heart take command of your life for a few days. If you think you are going in the right direction, go with it. Otherwise? Live truly, because you are the only one to judge your thoughts, actions and speech. Everything will change. Just take a step towards life, brothers and sisters.

Chapter 11

Benevolence (What Is, As It Is)

Claudine

French global citizen, female, early 70's, entrepreneur

Preface: Claudine is of an aristocratic background (a titled Baroness) and a Daughter of the British Empire, decorated for her charitable acts. I knew her only as "Madam Chapeau" (the hat lady) and the mother of my good friend Michelle. She is known, I am told, for her habit of wearing hats and traveling with a hat box (at least in the old days). We met in India recently just before Christmas and enjoyed time both at and away from the ashram, including holiday shopping and a tea party with carrot cake!

I first met Claudine at early morning meditation and was struck with her simple, classic style and the aura of sophistication and hint of glamour that follow her. I was present when she met her Master again after several years of not seeing him in person. The deep affection, trust, and respect between them were obvious, as was the love and devotion that connected them. I have rarely met anybody as dedicated and in touch with her spirituality. It is literally a guiding force in her life.

Claudine is second of three generations in Sahaj Marg and among the first preceptors to enter China. She has been active as a preceptor for nearly 20 years and shares her story through writing answers to my questions. She shares a story of pain, loss, anger, and eventual changes after starting the Sahaj Marg meditation practice. She helps us to better understand that we live in a world of duality and need the balance provided by no impressions, gained through unity. Claudine also describes and exemplifies the current of love that can pass between an abhyasi and the Master, leading to constant remembrance and connectedness. She focuses on a benevolence that can free us – from materiality, self-consciousness, anger – as we learn What Is, As It Is.

Kim: What is your background and how did you become interested in spirituality?

I was born in North Africa during the war. After my Dad passed away, from the age of nine to sixteen, I was sent far away to Dominican boarding schools from which I came back home only three times a year.

As far as I remember, I have always been conscious of the antinomy between the Christ spirit and with my daily life experience in a convent. There were hierarchical, elitist privileges for some and hard humble tasks for others. Rules were powerfully enforced. The pomp of the system and its inner contradictions [were obvious]. Therefore, I always had faith but I did not trust any religious system. I knew there was "something," a kind of irrefutable transcendent order, and I was determined to find out about it.

However, my first priority in life was to have a family and my second absolute goal was to get to the highest possible tax bracket! With my husband, I lived in Bahrain (the Persian Gulf) for four years at the end of the 1960's while travelling extensively in the Gulf. Then we moved to the U.S.A. with a newly-born baby girl and later had a boy. I studied Interior and Architectural design in Chicago and worked at restoring houses. We would live in the house while I was working on it, then sell and move on to the next project. I also worked as an antique dealer and trader in paintings in New York. My husband's job required constant travelling to Central America, India, and Madagascar so the family was often on the go. We moved back to Europe in the mid-1980's (France, Monaco, and Switzerland), then to Shanghai (P.R.C.) from 1996 to 2000. After that, I went back to Switzerland and am now retired in France.

I tell you all this so you can see the life style we led. Besides having to learn languages and becoming expert in packing, regular moves to foreign countries taught me lots of valuable lessons, one of them being to first agree on semantics. Languages are based on symbols, and concepts vary with latitude and longitude. Accordingly, what does "spirituality" mean? It comes from spirit. It can be anything from a mundane sense of spirit like "attitude" or "wit" to a volatile substance like alcohol, to a more vital sense like a "principle of life" or "God's breath." Similarly, my own evolution took me through experiencing the various meanings of the word "spirituality."

Early in my life, like most of us, I chose several roles (mother, wife, business woman, and socialite). I did my best to play my parts and to comply as closely as possible with my concept for each role. With time, those concepts crumbled. My experiences did not match the beauty of the concepts. I realized the price paid for high living standards was simply too high. We were generating expenditure that we had to work harder to maintain, while having less time to enjoy it. I felt my roles were mere facades and I did not like what I had become. I was in my late 30's and felt an urge to find meaning to it all. In the midst of an existential crisis, I decided to go to El Salvador, a country I knew well, stricken by civil war at the time. Trying to be useful to someone, I first visited patients in hospitals.

I met desperate people on hospital beds with awful wounds. Tortured, often left handicapped, each patient told me his story, while I cried. I only offered compassion and sympathy. However, there was a sparkle of hope in the eye of each person when I left, the shadow of a smile. Someone showing genuine interest in their distress was all it took. This miracle happened repeatedly, several times a day, every day. I felt "connected." The emptiness had gone.

Back home, for the first time, I had gratitude for our luxurious life style. Our move to Europe and a new renovation project hardly diverted me from my spiritual quest. I read esoteric literature. I went to conferences. I went to India and Turkey looking for guidance. And I often recited St. John of the Cross' poem:

"In spite of all the beauty
I will never give my soul away
Unless it is for something, I don't know
Which comes at random…"

It was at an official government reception that I was introduced to Sahaj Marg. Finally, my call had been heard! After my first introductory sitting, 30 years ago, I did not have the slightest doubt about giving my soul to the care of my Master. I have never regretted it.

Kim: How have you changed since you started this practice?

If Sahaj Marg had another name, it would be called "Constant Change." After practicing for only a few weeks, I felt some inner serenity. Having just faced a painful divorce, I found my spiritual practice did restore a broken heart and soothe a distressed nervous system. Each "sitting" taken with a preceptor engages a process of cleaning which is thought to be unique to Sahaj Marg. One feels lighter after each cleaning. After some time I could feel some detachment with my own self. I had become distanced from my own emotions, my own body and its suffering. In a way, I had become numb to my own life. The sharpness of the pain had gone, and also the bitterness. A new attitude emerged, a kind of benevolence towards what is – as it is.

The cleaning of tendencies can take us to a middle point: not this, nor that. It takes us to a balanced state. The purpose of cleaning is to remove tendencies, knowing that there are neither good tendencies nor bad ones. On Earth, we are in the domain of duality, half-positive, half-negative. We have light and shadow, day and night, good and bad. A thing and its opposite are part of the very same thing, like both sides of a coin. This realization brought tremendous changes in my life. For one thing, it ended endless discussions and fights because I realized one thing and its opposite can be equally right. I realized that, on Earth, we have no alternative because we are at the level of Duality. The solution must come from the domain of Unity.

During each meditation, I could feel the love of the Master pouring into my heart, giving me the feeling of being complete. For years, I fed on this energy, from one meditation to the other. One day, replete with that Love, I sent it back to the Master. Unknowingly, I had just set up a kind of transmission belt, or loop, that would work endlessly. I finally was connected to my Master; I constantly could receive His energy. This was a most important change in my life.

I felt unconditional love coming from my Master's heart. I had always been trying to please everyone because I desperately needed to be loved. In our world, loving someone usually means doing what he or she wants. Sometimes against my principles and often at the cost of a tremendous fatigue, I had complied with others' wishes. All of a sudden, my necessary vital need for love was covered. I could relax. Finally, I was sheltered and protected without being judged.

Of course, this realization had a big impact on my life. I became stricter to my principles. I could smilingly say "no" while sending out this love pouring into my own heart. My family and people working around me were beginning to say that meditation had tremendously improved my character. It also put an end to the everlasting romantic dream common to many women: finding the perfect man! I had found Divine Perfection in my Master. I could accept losing the mere illusion of a perfect husband.

The other change coming forth from my conscious connection to the Absolute was that I lost self-consciousness. Accustomed to judging ourselves based on the opinions of others, we can easily feel diminished by others' perceptions. I did not care any longer what people thought of me. Harsh judgment or compliment, both just flew over my head! As a socialite and successful business woman, I was very conscious of appearances. After decades of efforts to improve my own appearance, this new condition was extremely comfortable.

A more serious consequence of my change was a newly-acquired clarity of mind. Prior to writing a report or an important letter, I always pray for inspiration. Then, without any conscious thought process, with a mind perfectly quiet, like under dictation, I write. Later, I am always flabbergasted by the clarity of what has been written.

This is another miracle of Sahaj Marg – the transformation of an ordinary being into someone who can have access to a higher plane of consciousness by connecting to the Master. At His level, in the domain of Unity, there is no longer distortion of facts, amalgams (mixes), confusion between causes and effects, blindness to the solution, and so on.

With the years, I have also developed an inner voice which tells me what to do and, more importantly, what to avoid. It took a long time before I could trust it implicitly. For example, my voice would tell me to park elsewhere or I would get a parking ticket! My inner voice would tell me which deal would turn sour or which meeting would be a waste of time. The inner voice proved always to be right. It is, in fact, a big relief to obey inner orders. It saves long self-questioning and you can feel assured you have reached the right decision.

The last change that I have observed strikes me like a genetic change. People of my generation and younger generations are focused on seeking pleasures. This was a major part of my past life. Now, because of the slow transformation I have been undertaking over the years practicing Sahaj Marg, I have lost even the idea of what I like and dislike. I eat without asking myself whether it is good. When I have something to do, I do it, without checking whether I could do something more pleasant. My heart is connected to this wonderful flow of love coming from my Master's heart and the rest is trifle!

Accounting for all the changes I have experienced, I have to admit that all together I am another person. I feel I am living in a permanent state of Grace.

Kim: What advice would you give to someone new to the concept of spirituality or someone who is wondering about the purpose of life?

When looking for the purpose of life, we all look for an individual answer. I think we find the solution when conceived from a different outlook. To me, today, the meaning of life is to inhale a Divine Energy in an upper world and to exhale it in this world. Thus, I dissolve my own self-consciousness into that of the Absolute. I become oblivious to the roller coaster of life. I have entered the era of miracles, when Nature helps to a degree that people may think me mad when narrating some experiences.

Cancer is the individualization of the cell. In the same vein, we all have become ill since we forgot that each one of us is a cell of the human organism. Individually, at the cosmic scale, we are only an obnoxious illusion. We humans have reached such a degenerate stage, it takes decades to clean us up. We have lingered for so long in negativity, that whatever our efforts, by ourselves, we would never be able to come close to a pristine condition. Only a powerful Master can show the way and help reach it. For your own sake, take this chance!

Kim: How might this or similar practices change the world? Can it be considered a social movement? Does it bring hope for the future?

I do not know other practices. However, I am sure Sahaj Marg practice does change people. Therefore, if people change, the world will change.

Of course, spirituality brings hope for the future! Hope lies in change. We all know our civilization depends on coal, oil, nuclear energy, all of which are destructive both to humans and to the environment. Every day we are getting figures showing we are above the accepted limits of pollution. We already pay a heavy health price for the pollution we create. Alongside, we see wars everywhere, famines, and so on. Let us be happy that something is changing! Let us welcome change that will allow our children to have a future!

I trust Nature. Climate change has induced a process that will slowly force us to modify our habits and our way of living. Look at the marvelous generosity when people respond to a disaster to help their afflicted neighbors! The future will bring many of these opportunities.

Whatever we do towards spiritual evolution is firstly for our own benefit.

Kim: Do you have anything to add or any interesting or meaningful stories to tell from your personal experience with Master or with heart-based meditation?

My Master's teaching has answered every metaphysical question I ever had. All the pieces of the puzzle slowly fit, showing me the kinds of attitude and behavior I should have in order to suffer less and to evolve.

I was a widow before my twenty-second birthday. The grief was such that I tried to commit suicide. A few years later, I lost my first baby boy in Bahrain. Again, I felt the atrocious pain of a hemorrhaging heart, with every nerve ending naked. I was in despair. It took many months before I could see the sunshine again. The old question, "Why did it happen?" kept coming back. The anger was consuming, the heart frozen.

I think my heart reopened years later when I went to El Salvador. Bombs were exploding and there was no way to escape the proximity of death. I reconnected with my soul when I accepted death as part of the condition of life. I began to understand that our permanent abode is where we were before we were born and where we will return after we die. Life is only a breath. There might be something else to do with it than trying to always, "Have fun"! Everything began to make sense when I took life as a school for personal evolution.

After a few years with my Master, I began to see grief as a comprehension process. A toddler tumbles, falls, hurts himself, cries and gets back on his feet until he learns to walk. We adults experience pain until a Master teaches us God's non-circumventing Rules. My existential discomfort vanished only once I accepted those rules and started to obey them.

Kim: What final words or messages do you have for us?

 In our practice, during meditation, a transmission is sent from the Master's heart to the heart of the disciple, usually through the channel of a preceptor. To the beginner in Sahaj Marg, this transmission of Divine Energy is first a healing Energy for our dysfunctions. With time, the Divine Energy starts to function as an evolutionary motor, slowly increasing our vibration. The subtler a person's vibration, the higher the level of consciousness. A higher level of consciousness puts us in resonance with What Is, As It Is. Using a metaphor with water: "The drop of water loses its consciousness to obtain consciousness of the Ocean." This condition gives us both total faith and the joy of being securely guided to what is best for us. Of course, while being incarnated, we will never be able to understand the working wheels of the Universe because it is far beyond our grasp. We have not been programmed for it. Occasionally, however, we can peek at this Luminous World, and never be sorry for the trip!

We have been lured so often by promising commercials giving away all sorts of things which end up finally being useless and costly. As a result, we are suspicious when something vital and free is offered.

Nature is generous and free. I consider Sahaj Marg as Nature's gift to help humans out of their miseries. Thank you.

Chapter 12

From Lamb to Lion

Smriti

Indian, female, 40's, teacher

Preface: I first met Smriti at a birthday celebration bhandara in Tiruppur. She is best friends with my friend, so we all saved seats for each other at evening meditation and moved out of the huge tented meditation hallway together afterward, moving slowly through the crowd and looking for Smriti's two teenage children. Although we'd meditated together for hours, I hadn't spoken with her much besides talking about teaching (both our professions) and about parenting. I am eager to hear more about her in this interview and also intrigued when I learn she is a storyteller. My husband had been a professional storyteller and I wondered if it meant the same kind of work in her culture. We settled into our friend's living room, I adjusted the tape recorder and, within minutes, am enthralled. This is truly a master storyteller. Tears come to my eyes as she shares her feelings and experiences.

Moving from a successful career as a textbook editor to that of a teacher, Smriti shares with us how she helped to implement values-based spiritual education as part of her teaching career in two different school systems. She discusses her experiences as a Reiki healer and her introduction to Sahaj Marg, including her family's reactions when she decided to start Sahaj Marg meditation. She eventually made the difficult decision to move away from her extended family so that her children can attend and she can teach at Omega school nearby the Sahaj Marg mission headquarters. Smriti describes in poetic detail her interactions with her Master and his assurance that he is offering his protection while encouraging her to grow from being a "lamb" to being a "lion." This is a beautiful story of love, service and dedication told by a master storyteller.

Kim: I'd appreciate if you could start by telling a little about your background and how you became interested in spirituality?

I was born into a very traditional Hindu family. My grandparents and parents were deeply into Hindu ritualistic practices, but they never forced anything on me. So we had a religious life from the beginning with vegetarian food, going to the temple, keeping fasts and observing all the Hindu practices. From my childhood, even from when I was in the first grade, I learned a mantra called the Gayatri mantra. It's supposed to invoke the Almighty's grace for liberation, and I used to be chanting that all the time.

I was always looking for something beyond the emptiness but I didn't know what that was. There was a phase when I was connecting to any image of the Gods, especially Krishna – and then I turned to Shiva, both deities in Hinduism. Then I got into mantras more, some of them very difficult. One of them had a musical rhythm to it. It is said that God created it to please Lord Shiva and he acquired a lot of powers from it. So I was really mesmerized by that [the mantras] and they used to go on in me all the time. I was always craving perfection. I would always try to be top in my studies and top in my grades.

As it happened, I got married very early. My Dad found a real suitable guy. My father and my husband's father were friends and they met after a long time and decided to get their kids together. So, right after finishing tenth grade, I was just entering college and I got married. It was a huge digression to my spiritual development because I was completely head-over-heels infatuated, and it was a romantic rollercoaster fairy-tale life. But, how long can that last? After a few years, I was aggressively looking [for spirituality] again. By then I was about to graduate in my zoology college studies, was working on a dissertation in physiology and biochemistry, and felt a deep quest for intellectual satisfaction. My husband is a professor, so we used to have a lot of philosophical debates. I was looking for God in atoms and sub-atomic particles; and then when I got into cellular biology, I was looking for Him [there]. Is He there? Where is He?

After a time, I got to listening to discourses on the Bhagavad Gita, which is a part of the scriptures where Lord Krishna speaks and they talk about having a balanced life. The idea is to do the work without any expectation of the result, being in constant remembrance of God, and having a very stable mindset where there are no ups and downs or jagged emotions inside you. I used to wonder how that could possibly be done. How can we achieve that? They gave a technique called Kriya Yoga, so I was wondering where you find this Kriya Yoga? They have this idea that He is the omnipresent; He is the all-pervading substratum everywhere. It was really intriguing. I used to wonder where and how He is making the atoms and molecules, making the air.

Then I found Reiki, which is the Japanese technique of healing. A friend was introducing Reiki Master to her friends and most were full of curiosity about the power to heal somebody with their hands. I went with faith and, having done Reiki I, got embedded in the system. I was practicing it all the time and it gave miraculous results. What's really amazing is that you can send cosmic love [and] energy to somebody and he should feel healthy again; it was very strange. We had to then practice our own Reiki meditation to re-charge ourselves. That was one and a half hours of morning meditation.

So this habit of waking up early has been with me since childhood. It started with my studies; I would be up at four or five o'clock revising (reviewing my studies). Then I started this Reiki meditation, so it was easy. Then I got into Reiki II, which has a lot of Japanese chants and really intricate symbolism (recites part of a chant in Japanese). I was deeply into it and was doing it on everybody without anybody knowing it. I would go, "Please help this one and please help that one." It was a wonderful spree of being connected with Him and being able to just give, give, give.

I had a spate of illness in the family. My father-in-law was down with kidney failure that led to multi-organ failure. The doctors could do nothing more for him. In Hindu tradition, a daughter-in-law is not supposed to touch a father-in-law, but Reiki is about healing by touch so I sat next to him [to try to heal with Reiki]. I sat with him the whole night through with my husband there with us. I don't know what Reiki magic happened (God knows!) but in the morning, he said he was fine. The doctors didn't understand it and wondered if it was the cocktail of antibiotics they had given him. Anyway, it worked.

Then came my brother. He is an army officer and was up in the Kargil mountains where he slipped and fell, badly shattering his knee. Guys in the army need to be in A-grade fitness so I put my total focus on trying to heal him. He was my brother and it was so important that he should be fit. He was not healed and had to undergo surgery and a lot of trauma. I found myself extremely attached to the result and no longer saw myself as a fit instrument.

That [experience] disillusioned me from Reiki so I started looking again. My cousin was into Sahaj Marg. He said he was following a system of meditation that offers nothing. I could never understand it, the technical jargon. He said it was "transmission" and he said it offers you nothing. I asked him what he meant. He said it can give you luck. I asked him what that was, and he said it can give you not so good health, not a lot of money and perpetual criticism. I thought that was the way to being a saint; that was not so attractive. Then he had a backache that he wanted me to heal and I agreed. As I was healing him, I felt a lot of Reiki energy going into him. All he could tell me was that he felt a lot of transmission and that his Master was definitely working, but I could not understand that.

My cousins suggested I contact a preceptor so that he could help me do meditation. I was still attached to my Reiki meditations because they were full of light and sound effects. I could see vibrant colors of red and purple, and my body would just vaporize into atoms. I would sit there and feel an oncoming flu and I would be healed, so I really loved that meditation. I was wondering whether to try a new one [system of meditation] but then did call up the preceptor. He happened to live extremely close to my place. He called me and fixed an appointment, but I had better things to do (like have a party with my girlfriends), so I cancelled on him.

Luckily, thank God, I went there after a week and I sat there and wondered who was conning whom? Was I trying to read his condition – or was he trying to read mine? He said, "Okay, if you're ready, I can give you a sitting." So he gave me my first initiation and I expected it to be at least something like my Reiki meditation [but] it was just okay. I went again the following day and that was good. After the third sitting, he told me I was initiated and that I could do my own meditation practice on my own. I told him that I had been doing it on my own already, that I had been doing my one and a half hour Reiki meditation, and after that one hour of his meditation. He didn't say anything after that, thank God. He never told me you have to give up Reiki when you do this.

I carried on doing two and a half hours of meditation every day. One was Reiki, full of light and sound effects, where I could hear all with my heart and I could see vibrant colors. I was very tuned in to my intuitive powers and could immediately feel things happening in my heart, like when I told you about my brother's accident. Even before it happened, I could see it happening. In a way, this sharp intuition is painful. Friends would call me up and say, "Oh! I've lost my golden ring." I would tell them, "Well, it's under your sheet." Then they would call back and say, "How did you know?" I told a friend that she had a surprise party coming up and that her husband was going to invite 20 people. She called me back to tell me she was cooking like crazy because there were a whole lot of people at her house! It was unsettling to be so intuitive. I didn't like it because you have to feel the pain and are anticipating it; it's terrible.

After three months of my practice (I used to do my meditation, the cleaning, the nine o'clock prayer, the bedtime prayer), I was still waiting for something magical to happen in my meditations. My preceptor used to tell me that I had to get into constant remembrance but I would wonder where this was. I would go home and see my shadow, and wonder if that was Him? In my thoughts, I used to wonder where He was, as He was supposed to be with me all the time. I was really very curious about that. From the beginning, I realized I had to find this constant remembrance and do it. Actually, it was far easier doing the mantras because all you have to do is chant and you feel connected. With Reiki, you do the symbols. You do the chantings all the time and you feel, yeah, you're connected! And you definitely are because I could feel my hands on fire all the time. If there was anybody in the vicinity who was not well, I would feel my hands as iron-hot and I would want to heal him; many times the person wouldn't even know.

But I couldn't find out how to do this constant remembrance. Then my preceptor suggested that He is the one doing everything whenever you begin anything. So when I was brushing my teeth, I thought, "Uh-oh, Master's brushing" or when I had my first bite, I thought, "Uh-oh, Master's eating."

Kim: When you say Master, do you mean the physical Master or the ultimate God Master?

Now I have a different understanding of it. At that time, I must confess I thought physically, perhaps. I didn't have a clear understanding of it at that time. Then, I had the good fortune of attending a very special meeting where a prefect from Master's working committee came to the city. He gave us a sitting and he asked me directly if I had met the Master. When I said no, he said, "You need to go close to the fire to feel its warmth." Those words left me shattered, and I thought I just had to go and see him.

You have to remember that I belong to a very traditional family where all my in-laws are into traditional practices with all the pantheon of gods all over the house. According to my parents-in-law, I had already digressed a lot. They wondered where I vanished to every Sunday and every Wednesday [when I went to group meditation]. I broke all rules that a dutiful wife and obedient daughter-in-law should never, ever do. I bought tickets and went off to Calcutta to spend four days with my Master, against the wishes of all my friends and family.

When I was there, my heart was ready to burst. I reached Calcutta and was standing outside Master's cottage totally shivering, shaking like a leaf in a cyclone. An abhyasi came up and said, "What happened? Would you like some water?" He gave me some water to drink and I told him I was shaking because I am standing so close to the Master. "I've never seen him and I have no idea what he is like." He said, "Do you want to see him?" I said, "I can?" He replied, "Oh yes, follow me." and he took me right inside the cottage, where we sat and waited because the Master was resting. Then he took me right upstairs next to the bedroom. We sat there and we waited and waited. I could visualize him, having seen his picture.

I forgot to tell you – my cousin had given me a very precious book entitled My Master. He told me that, by the time I finish reading it and have a craving, the guru will come to me. So I read the book and, after my Reiki meditations, I would pray,

"Okay Guru, where are you? Would you please come to me?" with tears in my eyes. Perhaps that stepping-stone led me to Sahaj Marg.

So I was imagining pictures from the book, *My Master*. I remember how Master gave an account of his first meeting with his guru, about how deep his eyes were and when he looked into them he could feel eternity. He could not fathom the depth of those eyes. So I sat there, still literally shaking, when the door opened and they invited us in. There were a few people, maybe ten, sitting there. Then I saw the Master, the all-resplendent glory, so white, dazzling bright and big, enormous. And there I was, rather petite and small, with short hair and looking girlish. He looked at me so deep and penetrating. I was introduced, "Master, this is Smriti from Patna."

Master sort of angrily glared at me, "You need an introduction?" and I looked at him and thought, "Wow! He's known me forever!" All I could say was, "No, Master." I didn't know what I was in for, but his presence had completely overtaken me. My entire body was vibrating, complete with energy, and I thought, "What is Reiki compared to this?" After a few anecdotes, he said, "Let's start meditation." I was right in front of him, almost at his feet. I tell you, I still remember that sitting. I don't know if I can call it a profound meditation, but I felt I was just put into a space shuttle and shot off with no protective gear. I was completely rattled. It was a huge blast of transmission. I didn't know what happened to me. I felt my heart was back, forward, front ways. I still remember the immenseness of that whole thing. It finally ended. I was visibly shaking. He gave us some *prasad*, some blessed food, and we went.

The following day, he gave us a satsangh in the meditation hall in Calcutta. I was sitting in the aisle of the third row and, after the meditation, they announced there would be a cultural program by the children. As the chairs were being taken away, I thought, "Oh, that's all we get to see of him?" and I was flooded with tears. I don't know why. I wasn't feeling sad at all, but something within me was just melting away. Lo and behold, his chair was brought and put right next to me! Impolitely, I ignored the cultural program, turned sideways, and looked at him and looked at him and looked at him forever. There he was, sitting right next to me; me at his feet. I was crying copiously. I don't know where all those tears came from but my heart completely melted.

I saw a wound on his toe and was shocked. The Master has a wound on his toe! I had an immediate urgency to do Reiki on his toe but something inside told me, "You cannot do a thing like Reiki on the Master of the universe! No, that's not for him. It's too tiny for him, such a Master." At that moment, I left Reiki – or perhaps Reiki just shied away from me.

I just kept looking at him and kept crying and, all the while, the Master kindly kept looking at me. After that, people came up and gave him flowers and gifts. Somebody gave him a big bouquet of red roses, and he just gave me that entire bouquet. I was just mesmerized. Eventually, he got up and left and there I was sitting literally howling, crying like a three-year-old. I was overtaken, completely. Surprisingly, the hall was full of thousands of people and no one came to console me. I later learned in the books that, when your heart melts at seeing your Master, you're supposed to be left alone for his work to carry on. So that was evidently a profound cleaning he had done on me, perhaps erasing many past impressions.

As I told you, I was deeply into tradition and, besides chanting mantras and doing Reiki and other things, I used to observe a lot of fasts. On Mondays, I always fasted all my life – and also all the birthdays of the various deities that came throughout the year. It seems I used to observe a lot of fasts. The following day was my fast day so I had not eaten anything. The Master gave satsangh (meditation) and after that, he gave a little speech where he said, "Today happens to be the Bengali New Year and the food is very special prasad. Everyone is invited to eat." Uh-oh! That was a direct instruction to give up my fasting attitude. So there I left my Reiki, my inhibitions of crying in public and I also gave up fasting every Monday.

I returned to my city to answer a barrage of questions. My father-in-law said, "What came upon you? Where was the need to leave the house and go to an ashram? No woman does that. These are not the signs of a pious Hindu lady!" And my friends said, "Oh! Where have you been? What did you do? Did you fall in love with some strange guy or what have you been up to?" I answered truthfully but nobody was convinced.

The very day I returned, I got a very high fever, which I was not used to having since I was practicing Reiki every day over the past five years. I was surprised. There I was, sick and happy and I did not want to do Reiki at all – to the immense chagrin of my parents. My husband and my family were shocked. They said, "You will keep falling sick! Why don't you heal yourself?" I said, "No! I'm so happy with this! I don't need to."

I used to be a book editor with a national-level publishing house and I was working on textbooks for the eleventh and twelfth grades, mostly biology books because my favorite topics were genetics, molecular biology and DNA. I was always looking for answers in the replication, transmission and transcription of genes.

My doctor, lawyer and professor friends had begun a storytelling library for underprivileged children. In Patna, there are a lot of such children who could perhaps never own a book, so we all contributed our own children's books and bought others so that we had a library with a lot of books. Every Sunday, we would have a session at no charge for the kids from the neighborhood. Our own children and their friends from the public and convent schools were also welcome. So it was a mixed milieu of all sorts of children from all sorts of backgrounds. We would begin with a prayer and then I would get into storytelling. It was tremendous to do Sherlock Holmes, C. S. Lewis, Charles Dickens, *The Chronicles of Narnia* and the *Magic School Bus* series because we knew those kids would never read those books. Perhaps they could not afford it or reach the level of English required to actually assimilate the messages. My voice, modulation and expression drew in the children. There were a hundred kids waiting for me every Sunday.

Now that I was in Sahaj Marg, there was to be a big shift. I found out that Sahaj Marg has a research foundation, which deals with a very special thing for children called VBSE, Values-Based Spiritual Education. It draws its principles from the United Nations and they include things [concepts] like love and compassion, peace and justice, truth and wisdom, sharing, friendship and caring. These are all wonderful values that we want our children to have, but today all these things are sorely missing.

So my message shifted to telling stories that would have a values-based message at the end; and it went into active experiments. We would give them chocolates with the bright, shiny wrapper, and we would say, "Now this tells you what the chocolate has, all the ingredients, the company and everything." We would tell them that it is equivalent to an education with all our PhDs and Masters [degrees]. We would ask, "Can you eat the wrapper? When you peel off that wrapper, it's like beautiful jewelry. Can you eat that golden wrapper?" They would say, "No, ma'am." and we would say, "Okay, there goes the golden wrapper. There's the beautiful chocolate! Can we eat that?" "Yes, ma'am." "That's what it's all about, our beautiful soul. The most worthy thing within us is the soul, which is the same chocolate in every heart, no matter the wrapping." So in these simple ways we would try to pass messages on to the children. I was surprised that the children with their pure, open-minded souls could lap it up. They had no questions or objections to accepting things that could be explicitly shown with examples.

With my storytelling and the VBSE, I found a newfound love for children and a way to connect to them, passing on a message that there is much more waiting for them in life than just polishing their intellect in math, literacy and the sciences. Each subject has much more to offer. There came a huge shift in my professional life. I don't know how, but I was given an opening in a school. So, from my desk job of enjoying molecular biology textbooks, I jumped into teaching.

I worked in a school which is very demanding. It was one of a chain of public schools in Delhi (and all over the country) and they believe that teachers need to be on their toes. So I was on my feet the whole day, from 9 o'clock to 4 o'clock. I loved teaching primary level because I knew I could weave the lessons in with stories. I used to begin my lesson with a story and a quiet prayer, be it math or science or English. We have a beautiful prayer in the Mission and I introduced almost 500 children to it because I was teaching various classes. So, throughout the day, I had the privilege of touching these 500 children's hearts. I began from the school bus; the bus journey was almost 45 minutes: "Oh God, thou art the real goal of human life. We are but slaves of wishes putting bar to our advancement. Thou art the only God and power to bring us up to that stage." Together with me, all 45 kids in the bus would recite this, and I could see them change, their beautiful hearts blossoming. The prayer definitely did something to all of them.

The teacher's seat in the bus was right in front with a few seats facing her. I took children in batches, so five of them would come to me during the journey and I would tell them one story from the values-based spiritual education, of course. They loved it. Those kids who would jump and shout in the bus would ask, "Ma'am, can we have a story, please?" It was amazing. I could see my heart just opening and something would just burst out of this heart and envelope the bus, the road, the city and grow bigger and bigger. Don't ask me what that was. Perhaps it was a flow of love. The children loved it. After the story, I would look around and that beautiful transmission would lull them off to sleep. Almost half of them would be knocked out; it was so soothing for them.

Out of nowhere, so many kids would come rushing and embracing me, "Ma'am!" It was lovely – not only the ones I taught, but almost anyone who came in touch. I knew that had nothing to do with this little Smriti. It had to do with that big Master because I would hold on to him for dear life and carry him before me wherever I went and all that standing [on my feet] just went *whoosh*. It was no strain or pain at all because there was something done by him.

We also had the good fortune of touching the hearts of the teachers. Every Saturday we were invited to attend pedagogy seminars and I was chosen to conduct those seminars. Be it any topic, it was very easy to mold it to a Sahaj Marg way of life and bring in the Ten Maxims (see references). The importance of prayer in our life, through stories, through examples, we could show to the teachers. Definitely, when everything else fails, it is prayer that works as the unfailing means of success for a disciple. Many of them were touched by that. How is it that a simple way of living can actually help us shed the superfluity of life which keeps us unnecessarily distracted? It's like going to the fair with our Dad and we want to burst the balloons, we want to buy the coconut water, we want to buy the toys, we want to buy the bangles, we want the dresses – and there Dad is waiting. We have to return home.

When I did the seminars, there was a complete erasing of me. I was never there; it was always him speaking through me. I would definitely begin with a pious invitation to him: "Master, please take over. Whatever is meant to be said today, please go ahead and do that." Those seminars were interactive, involving heart-to-heart discussion with the teachers about disturbances in their personal lives as well as how they handled the children.

In my class, I had the privilege of handling two very special children. One was autistic and he needed special guidance. His parents had almost given up on giving him a normal schooling, but he blossomed like anything [in my class even though] I didn't do anything special. All I did was, whenever he came to me and wanted to hug me, I just allowed it. There was a flow of love and, perhaps through Master, I could bring myself to the children's level and feel the child in them. All these children became a part of me and it was just amazing to bring in our poems and stories. It was amazing that, just by shifting my focus from being a great teacher trying to achieve a great professional level, I instead just allowed love to flow through and Master to work through me. It was not by chance that, not only were they being taught the academics, but also along with it came in the values as well as all the applause and accolades they needed. Master allowed love to flow through, not only to 50 children in one classroom, but to 500 children. Whenever we had assembly with the entire school, it was amazing. I would close my eyes and imagine that he is there conducting the assembly and his love was flowing. All I could think and feel was, "Oh, may all these children, may all these teachers just turn to you and may they be filled with your love and your protection forever."

Kim: The principal was very impressed by you, of course?

The principal wanted me to hold more and more seminars, take up more special education classes and give special classes as a storyteller of values-based education to all the classes. I'm sure something of that sort happened even though I have now left that school and have joined a different school, the Master's school. They still call me and, even after two years of my having left that school, 500 children practice that Sahaj Marg prayer and they love it. They keep calling me on Teachers' Day and keep sending messages and they are still in touch. The principal still wants me to return.

Perhaps Master had different plans for me. When I came to Manapakkam, headquarters of the Sahaj Marg mission, I had the good fortune of meeting a preceptor who gave me a very strange sitting. We both felt I needed to be in Omega School, which is a school run by the Mission. But, how do we get in? You can't barge into a school and ask to be shown around! Also, my city is in the north and Chennai is in the south. I belong to a very traditional family where such a step is unheard of.

Soon after, however, we (myself and our two children) saw forms for entrance applications. I didn't even know it was entrance time. So we decided to take the admission forms, went in to meet the principal and asked if my two children could join the school. The principal invited us (You've come from so far away!) to take the entrance test immediately. My kids said, "We're on holiday and you want us to take a test?" But they took the test.

We returned to my city and I forgot all about the school – but then I got a call to say that the kids had been chosen and when are we going to join? My heart was shattered. How can I send my children to boarding school? What would I do without them? After a Wednesday satsangh, I must have had courage because I called the principal and asked her if she had a vacancy for a teacher. She said, "Yes! You're welcome!"

So when we had summer vacation in my school, we went to Chennai. My children took up admission in the school, I took up a teaching post in the school, and we all started living here. I have immense gratitude to my husband that he should have allowed us to come here because my parents, my in-laws and my friends all said, "You're crazy! Who does that?" I asked them to please let me give it a try.

It was a huge shift in my life when I came to Chennai. I've never looked after a house and kids all on my own. I was used to living in an extended family where things got done. All I had to care for previously was the kitchen, the meals and make sure the fridge was well-stocked. Now I was thrown into the open world.

I definitely had his protection because there was a brand-new flat rented just for me next to the school, all ready for us. The kids enjoyed it because, from a limited exposure previously, they now had a very cosmopolitan milieu to experience; their friends were French and German and from all over the world, for example. From my point of view, when I stepped into the school, I could totally feel it was like at the ashram. You have to go in there to feel the vibrations. The moment you close your eyes you feel you can slip into meditation, it is so charged. With an open heart, one can feel immense transmission flowing. Imagine those beautiful blessed angels [children] being nourished with that nectar of life! Not only did they have the best education, but also the values-based spiritual system – and of course, the spiritual guidance of the Master.

My two years in the Omega school here have been a gift. It is the merging of my material life, a livelihood, and my spiritual life (of which service is a major aspect). In fact, I feel it's no longer a matter of making a livelihood but rather making a life. So there it is. In Hindi we say, "What comes from the source goes back to the source." The salary Master gives me goes back to become the fee for the education of my children.

My experience with the children of Omega School has been amazing. Each of them have eyes sparkling like diamonds and hearts as open as an ocean, big and wide. Here, we begin with the Master's prayer – and the kids! You should see them! Some of them can barely sit straight; they just plonk down as if deep in meditation. We begin classes with the prayer.

I can easily draw a parallel between the way we are teaching them and the way Master guides us, [following] his design, his plan for us. He knows what is best for us. So, for each of us, he has a plan and it is a differentiated plan for each of us. There are measured doses of transmission, for example, perfect for each abhyasi.

Similarly, I learned to design a plan best suited to the needs of my learners, each of them getting their specific type of work sheets. [I also learned] not to teach them at all but rather just help them learn, to scratch the surface of their curiosity so they learn. Who am I to teach them? They already know so much and they are so open-hearted. I remember once there was a guest lecturer, a microbiologist speaking to them. For some reason, he asked them, "Do you think there are aliens in space?" They didn't say there were or there weren't. They said, "Well, we don't know. There could be." They are very open-minded.

To my surprise, I got the class [grade] three to handle, the seven- and eight-year-olds. I was with them all day teaching English, Hindi, the sciences, computers and yoga. Even when I substituted for Art, it was like a complete quenching of my intellectual pursuits. All I have been trying to learn just flows out. He is ridding me of all that unnecessary baggage in my intellect that I have carried. He is allowing it to flow through me – and the kids lap it all up.

Social Studies are all about Indian tradition and culture but teaching yoga was new to me, although I used to practice yoga when I was a teenager. Having come to Sahaj Marg, I understood that the five-path hatha yoga was actually devised by Patanjali who in later life was Babuji. It became easier for me because I would say, Please Babuji, take over and teach them what you want." The children could easily do all the yoga postures as they had already been doing it for a long time – not as tricks but as a complete union of the body, mind and soul. They could slip into it as a calm, peaceful union and not just take it as exercise.

Kim: So what's next for you?

I really don't know. I'm growing to a satiation point with my story-telling and with my scientific explanations. My love for writers Roald Dahl, J. K. Rowlings and C. S. Lewis is pouring, it's flowing. And my Hindi…I love to read Hindi storybooks and the children have learned that language also. I don't know what it was about me and yoga because that also got fulfilled. Everything I learned in life and everything I wanted to learn in life has been flowing through me and getting expression through the school. I feel immense attachment for the kids. Really. They are all pure, wonderful souls who are ultimately seeking spirituality.

We were taking them on a field trip to the St. Thomas Church and I tried to prepare them for what to expect, that we would go there and pray and perhaps pray to Jesus. There's a little girl who said, "But Ma'am, I see him every day in my heart." Now what can I possibly tell such a girl? So I feel I am the one who's learning. When I assess them and their learning, I feel I am the one who is getting assessed.

I'm now in my sixth year of Sahaj Marg practice and still every day I'm waiting, trying, struggling to do constant remembrance. With the children around me, I'm so fully focused and attached to the work. All of it is flowing. I sometimes wonder if I need to take a break and focus only on my soul because, ultimately, that's the goal: to merge and be in union with the Self and have him direct everything that goes through me.

After coming to Chennai, I again had the good fortune of meeting the Master. It was pouring [rain] and there were only six or seven people there, me amongst them. He looked deep in my eyes and said, "You're always attached. You're always exploited, but I'm there to protect you." He told me stories and he kept saying, "I'm there to protect you." As he said it, I could see it. I really am, as a woman, so attached to my husband, to my children, to the school and all those little ones that I have the privilege of learning with. Exploited? Definitely. As a woman who has been brought up in an Indian setting, we don't ever have the option of speaking up. So he wants me to change, and to change radically – to speak up and stand up for myself and not be a quiet lamb in the corner anymore [but rather] to be a lion. I feel there has been a complete overhaul of my entire personality. Through my meditations, he amazingly gives past life regressions, where we see our past life go through as in a movie. The setting is different, but we can recognize the people. Sometimes my husband is there, my colleagues are there, family and friends are there – and I see myself as the same attached, exploited person.

I have the great fortune of having turned consciously to spirituality. My goal is no more to achieve greatness in life by way of earning a lot, by being a great philosopher, being a great scientist or a great teacher – none of that. All those ambitions have been shed. I must have been so ambitious, getting top grades in college and working like crazy as an editor.

Perhaps a seven-day retreat would help me. Master says that those seven days are crucial. You focus only on going into your inner self, being in constant remembrance of the Master. When we meditate, he gives us a special condition. At the end of the meditation, when we brood over the condition of the heart, we can definitely feel there is a unique condition there. This cannot be spelled out in words. It's perhaps a very light feeling, a fluttering – or a deep feeling like a volcano has just erupted or perhaps a tremendous vibration as if each atom of the body could shatter. It depends. It's a unique condition for each meditation. We have to train ourselves to identify that condition. Afterwards, I tend to find that we have to learn to retain it and not to fritter it away like trying to clutch a handful of sand.

So how to retain it is a question I have been really wondering with my mind, but that's only intellect. My heart told me I've got to make it grow – grow and spread. So I'm going through a head-over-heels love for Master – not love in the way we think for a man and a woman; it's something else. It's an energy flowing through me. I can perceive the back of me, the sides of me, the front of me – and it grows and it grows; it's so subtle. Even when I take my journey home, from ashram to home or from anywhere in the city, it grows with me and flows into each heart that is there. If I'm in a bus, I see that the ambience changes and people just calm down and everything is quiet. It's something else, you know?

Even as I try to make it grow and keep it gathered with me, I feel by the time it's midday I do get distracted and it fritters away. So I definitely need to work on that and make it grow so big, hold on to it and hold on so tight, as a priceless treasure that can never leave me. Once that happens, there is that great knocking on his heart and he will definitely open the door and look at me and say, "Smriti, finally you have come to me."

So there's still the journey and perhaps I've taken a small step of fourteen inches, but his step will be great, from infinity towards me. So that's what I'm waiting for, his big step towards me.

While I go through life each day, full of upheavals, turmoil, disturbances, I know he protects me. I know I can go through it. I can sail through it because it doesn't take me over completely and devour me in its sorrow and complexity. As Master has promised, he protects me like a kangaroo, with me as a child in his pouch.

Conclusion

We've been given much to feel, think about and learn in these stories. Many thanks again to the interviewees for sharing such personal, important thoughts. Dear readers, I hope you agree we have met a number of extraordinary people, people who are orienting their lives and their goals around spiritual evolution. A recurrent theme many share is that, through changing ourselves, we can change the world. This provides a great deal of hope and a pathway to making our world a better place and our lives more meaningful. We are also reminded to think of humanity as one organism, each of us like a drop of water with the ability to coalesce and merge. The ocean awaits as we individually and together journey within and beyond.

It has been an amazing and incredibly fulfilling experience to meet these people and others involved with the writing of this and the first book of this series, The Journey Within: Extraordinary conversations with uncommon people. A newcomer with many questions about the practice, I appreciated hearing various explanations of concepts that were somewhat mystifying. We heard many stories of principles being put into practice, stories of courage, trust and dedication. We are also given valuable advice. For example, while working on character development, we are encouraged to avoid putting undue pressure on ourselves as that only strengthens impressions. We are reminded that this is the Natural Path. Change is subtle (like the unfolding or blossoming of a flower) and comes naturally if we do the practice with love, joy and dedication.

In this book, many if not most of the interviewees are preceptors, or prefects. They explain aspects of the practice as well as their own challenges and personal goals. Through them, it is easy to gain a deeper personal appreciation for the value of the practice itself. Similar to what others describe in the book, I feel more balanced and less concerned with daily events that used to affect me. I can practice patience, tolerance, and love for others. I am more happy with "what is as it is." I try to speak less and I try not to be critical. I work hard to control my thoughts, try to not even think at all but rather listen to the heart. There are changes in those around me, so behavior and lifestyle changes can affect others in a positive way. I am beginning to understand our role in breathing in the divine energy and radiating it around us as we develop and practice constant remembrance and stay connected to the essence within.

Many in this book talk about "the journey" of Sahaj Marg and the fact that it requires a great deal of hard work. Some talk about a long-time search for a guru and all speak touchingly of the role of the Master in the evolutionary process. We are encouraged to surrender and to listen to our hearts and inner voices so as to more easily learn and grow during the relatively short time we have in this lifetime. That was my purpose in writing this book. It seems to me these voices need to be heard. All our dear sisters and brothers, from around our globe (and beyond!), imagine all of us growing in faith and in love. May you successfully seek, be fulfilled, and evolve as you follow your own journeys within and beyond. Please share this book with others if you find it valuable.

References and Resources

Alfassa, Mirra (1878-1973). Affectionately known as "The Mother" by many living at Auroville. More information can be found at http://www.auroville.org/vision/ma.htm.

Amar Chitra Katha. Please refer to http://www.amarchitrakatha.com/ack/

Asimov, Isaac (1951). The Foundation Trilogy: Three Classics of Science Fiction. Garden City, NY: Doubleday.

Babuji Maharaj, also known as Ram Chandra of Shahjahanpur, founder president of Shri Ram Chandra Mission (SRCM).http://www.sahajmarg.org/babuji-maharaj

Bhagavad Gita in English is available at http://www.bhagavad-gita.org/index-english.html
Cambridge Centre for the Study of Existential Risk. Please refer tohttp://cser.org/

Chandra, Shri Ram (2010). Whispers from The Brighter World - A Third Revelation. Rajagopalachari, P. (Ed). Spiritual Hierarchy Publication Trust for Sahaj Marg Spirituality Foundation, Kolkata, India.

Chandra, Shri Ram (2012). Whispers from The Brighter World - A Fourth Revelation. Rajagopalachari, P. (Ed). Spiritual Hierarchy Publication Trust for Sahaj Marg Spirituality Foundation, Kolkata, India.

Chandra, Shri Ram (2013). Whispers from The Brighter World - A Fifth Revelation. Rajagopalachari, P. (Ed). Spiritual Hierarchy Publication Trust for Sahaj Marg Spirituality Foundation, Chennai, India.

Chariji Maharaj, Revered Parthasarathi Rajagopalachari (1927 - 2014). For more information, please see
https://www.sahajmarg.org/chariji

Chinmayananda, Swami (1916-1993). Hindu spiritual leader and teacher. For more information, please see
https://www.mychinmaya.org/index.php?id=art_gdbiography

Constant Remembrance, the global spiritual quarterly magazine of the Shri Ram Chandra Mission:
https://www.sahajmarg.org/publications/bookstore/constant-remembrance

Crown Chakra. See
http://healing.about.com/cs/chakras/a/chakra7.htm

Durga Chalisa. See
http://greenmesg.org/mantras_slokas/devi_durga-durga_chalisa.php

Gibran, Khalil (1883-1931). A Lebanese artist, poet, and writer who immigrated with his family to the United States as a young man. One of his first well-known books is The Prophet (1923).

Gita, Bhagavad. A 700-verse scripture that is part of the Hindu epic Mahabharata. It is a sacred text of the Hindus. Please see
http://www.bhagavad-gita.org/

Goenka (1924-2013). Satya Narayan Goenka was a noted Burmese-Indian teacher of Vipassanā meditation.
Seehttp://www.dhamma.org/en/about/goenka

Hafiz or Hafez (1325-26 to 1389-90). His works are regarded as a pinnacle of Persian literature and are to be found in the homes of most people in Iran and Afghanistan, who learn his poems by heart and use them as proverbs and sayings to this day. See

http://en.wikipedia.org/wiki/Hafezand
http://www.iranonline.com/literature/index-hafez.html

Hanuman Chalisa is a Hindu devotional hymn addressed
to Hanuman, a vanara (monkey-like humanoid deity), and
devotee of Rama. The word "chālīsā" is derived from "chālīs",
which means "40" in Hindi, as the Hanuman Chalisa has 40
verses excluding the couplets at beginning and end. See
http://en.wikipedia.org/wiki/Hanuman_Chalisa

Hatha Yoga, Five Points. See
http://www.sivananda.org/teachings/fivepoints.html

Krishnamurti, Jiddu (1895-1986). Speaker and prolific writer on
philosophical and spiritual subjects. Please see
http://www.jkrishnamurti.org/default.php for more details.

Kriya Yoga. See http://www.kriya.org/ or
http://en.wikipedia.org/wiki/Kriya_Yoga

Lalaji Maharaj (1873-1931). Also known as Shri Ram Chandra
of Fatehgarb, is adi-guru (first spiritual master) of Shri Ram
Chandra Mission.

Matrimandir, a structure called the "soul of the city" of
Auroville. For more information, go to
http://www.auroville.org/thecity/matrimandir/mm_main.htm

Oxford University's Future of Humanity Institute. For more
information, please go to http://www.fhi.ox.ac.uk/

Paramhansa, Ramakrishna (1836-1886). More information can
be found at http://www.om-
guru.com/html/saints/ramakrishna.html

Prayer, Night Prayer Meditation see
http://www.sahajmarg.org/resources/clarifications/night-prayer-meditation

Rajagopalachari, Shri Parthasarathi (1989) My Master. Kolkata: Spiritual Hierarchy Publication Trust.

Rajagopalachari, Shri Parthasarathi (2005). HeartSpeak 2005. Chapter on Existence, Consciousness, Bliss. Kolkata: Spiritual Hierarchy Publication Trust.

Ramakrishna (1836-1886). Born Gadadhar Chattopadhyay, Ramakrishna was a famous mystic of 19th-century India. A chief disciple was Swami Vivekananda. For more detail, see http://www.om-guru.com/html/saints/ramakrishna.html

Rampa, Lobsang (1956). The Third Eye. See http://www.lobsangrampa.org/data/The_Third_Eye.pdf

Reiki. More information can be found at http://www.reiki.org/faq/whatisreiki.html

Rumi (1207-1273). Jalāl ad-Dīn Muhammad Balkhī, also known as Jalāl ad-Dīn Muhammad Rūmī, Mawlānā or Molānā, Mawlawī or Molavi, and more popularly in the English-speaking world simply as Rumi, was a 13th-century Persian poet, jurist, theologian, and Sufi mystic. From http://en.wikipedia.org/wiki/Rumi

Saadi (1210 to 1291-92). Abū-Muhammad Muslih al-Dīn bin Abdallāh Shīrāzī, Saadi Shirazi, better known by his pen-name as Sa'dī or simply Saadi, was one of the major Persian poets of the medieval period. He is recognized for the quality of his writings and for the depth of his social and moral thoughts. See http://en.wikipedia.org/wiki/Saadi_Shiraziand http://www.iranchamber.com/literature/saadi/saadi.php

Saint-Exupéry, Antoine de. (1943). The Little Prince.

Sahaj Marg (Natural Path) Raja Yoga meditation. See
http://www.sahajmarg.org

Sufism. A branch of mystical Islamic belief and practice in which
Muslims seek to find the truth of divine love and knowledge
through direct personal experience of God. Information found
at
http://global.britannica.com/EBchecked/topic/571823/Sufism

The Ten Maxims can be found at
https://www.sahajmarg.org/sm/practice/ten-maxims

The Tibetan Book of the Dead (Evans-Wentz, 1927) based on
Bardo Thodol (8th century). Pdf version can be found at
http://www.holybooks.com/wp-content/uploads/The-Tibetan-
Book-of-the-Dead.pdf

Tolle, Eckhart (2004). The Power of Now. See sample quotes at
http://www.goodreads.com/work/quotes/840520-the-power-
of-now-a-guide-to-spiritual-enlightenment

Vedanta, the Upanishads, a collection of foundational texts
in Hinduism. By the 8th century, it came to mean all
philosophical traditions concerned with interpreting the three
basic texts of Hinduist philosophy. See
http://en.wikipedia.org/wiki/Vedanta

Vipassana is one of India's most ancient meditation techniques.
It was rediscovered 2500 years ago by Gotama the Buddha, and
is the essence of what he practiced and taught during his forty-
five year ministry. See http://www.vridhamma.org/VRI-
Introduction More information is available at
http://www.vridhamma.org/VRI-Introduction

Vivekananda, Swami born Narendra Nath Datta (1863-1902). Credited with raising interfaith awareness and bringing Hinduism to the status of a major world religion during the late 19th century. More details can be found at http://en.wikipedia.org/wiki/Vivekananda

Worthy, Martin (in production). <u>To Be All A Man Can Be.</u>